GIVE TO PROFIT

How to Grow Your Business by Supporting Charities and Social Causes

ALISOUN MACKENZIE

G2P Publishing

Published in 2017 by G2P Publishing

ISBN Paperback: - 978-0-9930752-2-3
Ebook: - 978-0-9930752-3-0

A CIP catalogue copy of this book can be found in the British Library.

Cover design by Sian Harris
Graphics by Sian Harris and Deanna Everett

Published with the help of Indie Authors World

IndieAuthors
World

Contents

Part 1 – The Give-to-Profit Business Model

Part 2 – Give-to-Profit in Practice

Introduction

"Do good, have fun and the money will come."

RICHARD BRANSON, VISIONARY ENTREPRENEUR

WOW, how did I end up here? Standing in an orphanage at the top of a mountain in Rwanda, in front of a sea of unfamiliar faces looking at me.

Watching. Eagerly waiting for me to start.

I'm way outside my comfort zone!

Only a few weeks ago I was running a successful training consultancy business spending most of my time delivering training courses in workplaces. But now I'm in a very different world, and unsure what to do.

The shy little child inside, who used to blush whenever anyone spoke to her, feels like she's gate-crashed someone else's party. With no idea if she's going to pull it off.

- What are they thinking?

- What are they expecting?

- What if what I do at home, doesn't work here?

All sorts of doubts are flying around inside my head, as I stand here feeling alone and uncertain about what is going to happen next.

Meeting the group of young genocide survivors for the first time, a few minutes earlier, had been easy. In fact it had been a wonderful uplifting experience to start the day with African singing and dancing to improvised drumbeats on a bucket, before a few minutes of prayer.

But now they are waiting for me to start today's training...

It was just three months ago that I set the intention to do something more meaningful with my life.

For the last few years I'd really enjoyed building my business but felt I'd become a slave to the job I'd created; and had very different values to some of my clients. Yes I loved what I did but my business wasn't providing the lifestyle I'd envisaged. I may have been earning good money but I was working too many hours, travelling a lot and felt there was something missing.

Whenever I saw films of people suffering around the world due to conflicts or natural disasters I'd feel useless – because I didn't think there was anything I could do: I wasn't a fire-woman, doctor, nurse or builder who could go and help.

Yes I regularly send money through disaster relief charities, as I know that's the best way to get what's most critically needed to those suffering. But I've always wanted to do more to save lives.

I remember vividly the day I walked away from a lucrative corporate training contract and decided to volunteer overseas.

At that stage I had no idea charitable giving and supporting social causes would become a core part of my business in the way it has. My initial intention was simply to 'give back'. I knew I wanted to support young people (as I hadn't been fortunate enough to have my own children); I wanted to use my skills; and to feed my passion for travel. I was looking for a meaningful break and adventure.

As often happens when you stop doing something that drains your energy, and get clear on what you'd like instead, opportunities appear. That's what happened for me.

The very next day I received an email with a link to a short film about a project in Rwanda helping young genocide survivors. Being someone who believes in synchronicity rather than coincidences, I took this to be a 'sign' and immediately sent an email saying, "I love what you're doing in Rwanda and would like to hear more".

Little did I know then how pressing 'send' that day would profoundly change the rest of my life.

I got an immediate response from the founder of the charity, Dr Lori Leyden, and we spoke a couple of days later. During that first conversation she invited me to join her in Rwanda in a few weeks' time. I knew the best way for me to suss out which charity to support was to experience their work. But I already had work commitments that clashed with the dates of the trip.

Surely if it had been right for me, the dates would have worked?

Wouldn't they?

Over the next few weeks Lori and I continued to chat and share ideas and not surprisingly my diary started to clear. That's how I found myself up the top of a mountain shortly after.

I'd intended my participation in the project to be a one-off trip followed by fundraising on their behalf – that if I liked the work they were doing, I'd start to donate a percentage of my profits to them each year. But during that first trip my heart burst open with love, and unleashed a desire to help that was so strong I couldn't walk away.

Without a doubt deciding to get actively involved with regular trips to Rwanda, rather than just donating money, has been one of the best decisions I've ever made – in so many ways.

It has completely changed the core essence of who I feel I am. After that first trip, I felt more connected to the authentic person I was born to be than I could ever remember. As someone who hasn't had my own children I now feel a deeper sense of meaning in my life, as well as more peace and contentment.

It's also been wonderful to meet all the amazing souls we support in Rwanda and all those connected to the project; I have a much broader perspective on the challenges of war, as well as the capacity we all have as human beings to survive, heal and love. I've also learned new skills and have all sorts of new interests thanks to what I've been introduced to by others.

All that feels great and would have been plenty but that is not all. One of the biggest surprises has been the impact on my business over the last five years. Here are just a few of the unexpected benefits I've experienced:

- I decided to remodel my business, to free up more time and money for me to do more humanitarian work. This was one of the main reasons I decided to step back from my workplace training consultancy, to start serving heart-centered business owners and social entrepreneurs, and to take some of my business online.

- My desire to raise funds for charity (I've raised over US$25,000 so far) has created all sorts of new opportunities for my business too – resulting in clients, business partners, contacts and additional income I would not otherwise have had.

- Being actively involved with the charity also helps me continually push through my comfort-zone, and try out new things I would previously have backed out of.

- My network has expanded greatly to include a host of like-minded and fascinating change-makers and thought-leaders. Many of whom I would have been unlikely to get to know had I not being doing my charitable work. Yet now we're connected because of common goals or values.

- Many people think I have an interesting story to tell which means I am invited to do talks and give interviews around the world – again these are great opportunities to help others and share my message with a wider audience.

- The personal transformations of those we support in Rwanda inspired me to write my first book Heartatude: The 9 Principles of Heart-Centered Success, and greatly influenced its content.

- Others ask me to help them decide whether they too could grow their business by supporting social causes through their business – as they've seen me do.

  This is the reason why I've written this book, and have created related products and services. These weren't planned but are welcome opportunities, feeding a bigger ripple of change around world, while boosting my social impact and personal income too.

Since you're reading this book I assume you're a business owner, entrepreneur, leader or change-maker who wants to make a difference in the world through your business.

You're likely to value giving back and helping those in need (whether people, wildlife or the planet). And you probably support charities, non-profits or social causes personally already.

The main purpose of this book is to show you how to grow a socially conscious business authentically and ethically by supporting a charities or social causes.

Supporting social causes is a great way to GROW your business. There are lots of quick and easy ways to do this, no matter what stage of business you're at, without needing to set up a charity, foundation or social enterprise with all the legal and organisational considerations that this involves.

Contrary to common belief, you don't need to wait until you earn money from your business before you support social causes. Likewise, keeping your business and personal giving separate could be costing you time and money.

Some people question whether supporting charities to get business is ethical. My opinion is that if you're only considering doing this as a way to get clients or make money, what I share in this book isn't for you – unless you're open to being more kind, loving and compassionate in your business.

To me, we all have a responsibility to support those in need. There are plenty people making an honest living from working for charities and social causes. Others volunteer or raise funds in their own time. And if you want to support a social cause through your business that's fine too. Remember, charities and social causes desperately need your support.

By reading this book you'll learn a huge range of ways to support charities and social causes through your business. Plus how to implement ideas best aligned to what is important to you and your business goals.

My aim is to help you implement ideas that engage your heart, add meaning to your life and grow your business. These could include: fundraising, volunteering, tithing (giving 10% of sales or profits to charity), and sourcing social suppliers. You may decide to do a one-off project or to put charitable giving at the heart of your business as I've done. There is no right or wrong. You can decide what will best work for you.

While my initial intention was to raise as much money as I could for Project LIGHT Rwanda, my charitable giving has evolved to a point where social impact is now a major component of most business decisions I make, including: how I select new business partners; how I launch or market my products and services; the marketing strategies I use; which networks I attend; what I offer; the suppliers I choose; how I tackle business challenges; and as part of my business planning. Without the charitable component, I'd now feel completely disconnected from my business.

I encourage you to think big and be creative when coming up with ideas, even if you don't know how these will manifest – yet.

I invite you to be open to the possibility that all sorts of wonderful opportunities will present themselves once you embark upon this journey. Yes, challenges may appear too, but I invite you to trust you'll be able to navigate your way through these, and that your efforts will be worth it.

Whether you're an established business owner, entrepreneur, or at the early stages of exploring a business idea, what I share will help you have a positive social impact through your business.

How to get the most from this book

This book has been designed so that you can either read it from start to finish (if this topic is new to you) or, if you've already got some experience of supporting social causes through your business, you can dip in and out of relevant chapters.

Part 1 – The Give-to-Profit Business Model

Discover why supporting charities and social causes is good for business, and the many ways to grow your business by doing so.

Part 2 – Give-to-Profit in Practice

Be inspired by fifty-two ways to raise funds for social causes through your business; become aware of potential legal obligations and best practices when doing this; and learn how to have social impact without spending any extra time or money by 'buying social'.

Part 3 – The Seven Steps to Grow Your Business by Supporting Charities and Social Causes

Follow a logical approach to coming up with and implementing charitable ideas that will have a positive impact on your business, your clients and the causes you'd like to support. This includes choosing a cause to support if you don't already have one in mind.

Download your free Give-to-Profit Practical Guide

Make it easier to implement your ideas by completing the Give-to-Profit Practical Guide that accompanies this book. You can download this for free at www.givetoprofit.com.

I hope you enjoy this book and wish you every success in implementing your ideas. Together we really can make the world a better place!

Alisoun x

March 2017

Your Invitation to Connect

I'd love to hear your thoughts, questions and success stories.

Check out www.alisoun.com for details of how to connect with me, get support or have me speak at one of your events.

PART 1

The Give-to-Profit Business Model

"If you organise your life around your passion, you can turn your passion into your story and then turn your story into something bigger – something that matters."

Blake Mycoskie,
SOCIAL ENTREPRENEUR and FOUNDER of TOMS SHOES

Ten Good Reasons to Support Social Causes Through Your Business

"Social change brings about clear, positive impact and business provides the means to do so."

MARC KIELBURGER, CO-FOUNDER of FROM ME to WE

1. **You'll touch the lives of more people**

    If you like to help others or are motivated to make a difference, supporting charities or social causes through your business is an easy way to do this and be of greater service.

2. **It's a great way to GROW your business**

    You don't need to wait until you have money to support social causes. In fact, strategically linking your business and charitable giving in the ways I share in this book, will help you grow your business, so you can immediately have more social impact and turn your business into a force for good.

3. Charities and social causes need you

Around the world, countries, communities, and individuals are increasingly relying upon charities, social projects and volunteers to provide critical services. There are plenty of charities and social causes who desperately need your help and would appreciate your support.

4. Consumers prefer businesses who care

There is a growing trend in socially conscious consumers who choose to buy from businesses who demonstrate they care about social impact as well as making a profit.

You don't need to leave your heart at the door of your business. In fact the sustainability of your business is dependent upon your ability to be human, connect to your heart and demonstrate to others that you care.

This is important particularly if your customers include Millennials (those born roughly between 1980–1995) or Generation Z (the cohort after Millennials). The 2006 Cone Millennial Cause Study [1], revealed some startling findings it would be beneficial for all businesses serving these markets to heed:

- 89% of respondents said they'd be likely to "switch from one brand to another (if price and quality are equal), if the second supports a cause."

- 83% said they'd be more likely to trust a company if it is socially and/or environmentally responsible.

- 68% considered a company's social and/or environmental commitment when deciding whom to buy from.

1 - 2006 Cone Millennial Cause Study, p10

- 45% were likely not to buy from companies that were not socially or environmentally conscious.

When you support causes (as well as delivering good products/services) people are more likely to buy from you and recommend you to others.

5. **Attract, engage and retain staff with similar values**

    In a similar way that younger generations are choosing to buy from companies who do good, many have similar considerations when it comes to who to work for. And as you'll soon discover there are many ways social giving activities can be incorporated into staff engagement programs. The more you integrate social impact into your business, the greater the potential for creating opportunities that attract and retain people with similar values.

6. **You'll expand your network**

    When you get involved in charitable activities you'll meet more people who share your values. Building relationships based on common values and strong emotional bonds often lead to more meaningful relationships, friendships, business partners and clients.

    When you support causes and connect with others because you have a passion for a similar cause, you'll also find doors open that wouldn't otherwise. If people like what you're doing, they'll want to support you and your cause, irrespective of who they are.

    You'll also build a community of followers, clients, collaborators, and partners who resonate with your vision, message and brand.

7. Memorable stories sell

With so many people marketing their products and services
it can sometimes be a challenge to be unique, stand out
or be memorable. However, when you support a charity
or social cause, and put this at the heart of your business,
this becomes part of your story, a reflection of your values
and your brand. People who relate to this are more likely to
feel a sense of connection and gravitate towards you and
remember you. You're also more likely to get free media
coverage. When it comes to getting clients, people work
with, promote and buy from those they know, like and trust.
My clients and I have found that having a charitable story
speeds up this 'know, like and trust factor' resulting in some
people becoming customers more quickly than otherwise.

8. You'll find it easier to charge good market rates

It may sound mad but I meet too many people trying to build
successful businesses helping those who can't afford their
products and services, especially well-being and personal
development professionals – but this is a sure way to fail in
business! If you struggle with charging good market rates,
contrary to what you may feel, you don't need to choose
between getting paid well and serving those who need your
help but can't afford it. It's possible to do both by selling
products and services to those who will pay you well for
them, and to develop a different strategy for supporting
those who can't afford them. The Give-to-Profit model
enables you to do this.

As soon as I decided do humanitarian work in Rwanda,
I felt connected to a much greater sense of purpose and
found it easier to split my time between well paid work, and
helping those most in need. Having these clear boundaries

in place, makes it much easier to say 'no' nicely to those who can't afford my higher priced services (there are free and low cost solutions they can access), and the time I spend doing unpaid work is with people and projects closest to my heart.

9. **Kindness is good for you**

As I talk about in my book *Heartatude, The 9 Principles for Heart-Centered Success,* there are many scientific studies which evidence that when we are kind we are more likely to be happier, healthier and even look younger.

Supporting a charity or social cause that's close to your heart or resonates with your values will also give you a deeper sense of purpose, satisfaction, and meaning – both personally and for your business. This often evolves and deepens as you form new connections with fellow 'difference-makers' and have more experiences together.

Have you ever found it easier to do something when you are doing it for someone else rather than for yourself? Whenever I've aligned what I'm about to do, to my desire to 'help the young people in Rwanda' I've found it easier to overcome mindset blocks and explore what's on other side of my comfort-zone. Learning and experiencing things you wouldn't have done otherwise also gives you a different perspective on how you respond to events.

I know that how I now think, feel and act in response to human tragedies such as the current Syrian Refugee Crisis in Europe is greatly influenced by my experiences in Rwanda. I'm more likely to take practical action now, as well as donate money.

The more you get involved in charitable activities, the more you will grow as a person and feel good about yourself.

10. **Supporting social causes through your business is EASY and could save you TIME and MONEY**

Many people think they need to set up a charity, social enterprise or foundation to operate a business with a social mission. But there's a much easier way to do this – the Give-to-Profit model that links business and charitable goals strategically.

Setting up a charity, foundation or social enterprise may open up funding opportunities, and be the right solution for many, but running this type of organisation comes with the extra burdens of additional legislation, needing others to be involved (for example having a board of directors or trustees), and potential trading restrictions. These structures may also not be suitable models even if you want to grow a business with a charitable or social mission.

The Give-to-Profit model in this book is a much simpler way to enjoy having the freedom to run a commercial business as you like, while also having a social mission and impact. It's an easier, more flexible, way to have social impact than setting up a charity or social enterprise.

I also have clients who have wanted to support charities while they were growing their business but didn't think they had time to do both until I showed them how to link the two strategically, as you'll discover later in the book.

If any of these reasons resonates with you, this book is definitely for you!

2

The Give-to-Profit Business Model

"An enterprising business model for business owners and social entrepreneurs who want to turn their passions into profits and make a difference in the world."

ALISOUN MACKENZIE

Most business owners and entrepreneurs I meet already support charities personally but don't realise the huge benefits (for themselves and others), of supporting social causes through their business.

Some make occasional donations of money or pledges of support through their business but haven't formalised how they'd like to do this regularly. Many are waiting until they've got the money to do so. Others would love to run a socially responsible business but don't know how to do this without going through the red tape of setting up a formal charity, foundation, social enterprise or B Corp. This isn't a surprise when most business training courses and books teach you how to set up a commercial business, social enterprise or charity. Only occasionally is it suggested in these formal settings that you can set up a commercial business that puts social impact at its heart. Rarely do people teach you how to do this.

> *"If you think you're too small to have an impact, try going
> to bed with a mosquito."*
> ANITA RODDICK, FOUNDER of THE BODY SHOP

I'm often asked why I don't set up my own charity or social enterprise when such vehicles exist. While I've sat on the boards of both types of organisations and I'm an avid fundraiser, the main reason I've not gone down that route myself is that I don't want to have to deal with all the extra restraints, legislation, and limitations that come with these types of organisations. I do very much want to have a positive social impact through my work but I prefer having the freedom to run a commercial business in the way I like, and to support different social causes through this.

Strategically linking your business to social causes, in the way I share in this book will mean you too can have more social impact, your business will grow as a consequence, and you'll have more flexibility to support a range of causes because you're not tied down to a particular charitable or social 'mission'.

Misconceptions about charitable giving

Before explaining what I mean by Give-to-Profit let's consider some common misconceptions about supporting social causes through a business:

MISCONCEPTION #01: MONEY: 'I need to wait until I have money before supporting a charity or social cause'

Many people who want to support social causes through their business but are not yet doing this, say a lack of money is the reason why. They're waiting until they have 'extra' money to donate. I used to think I needed to have enough money to pay myself first too, until my experience taught me the opposite is true.

This misconception stems from the mind-set that supporting charities and social causes is about giving back, for example donating 10% of sales to charity – only once we've got ourselves sorted. Yet as you'll discover there are many other ways to support social causes.

As I've travelled around the world I've experienced the incredible generosity of people who, according to Western measures of success, have nothing. They may have less but many seem more connected

You can start supporting social causes from the moment you set up in business.

to the essence of being human, giving of themselves and willing to share the little they have. As you'll discover shortly, there are many other ways you can support social causes other than making financial donations so you don't need to wait until you have money (see Chapter 3). And if you link your charitable giving and business activities strategically, as I teach in this book, you could generate more revenue, save money and have social impact in the course of being in business.

I'm not a fan of the phrase 'giving back' as it can have egotistical or 'pity' energy associated with it, that implies those who give are in some way above or better than those they give to. As though those with higher bank balances are superior to others. What naïve and uncompassionate nonsense!

The notion of 'giving back' also encourages us to wait until we have money before giving to others. But that's a fear-based approach to money, which isn't empowering and keeps financial abundance at bay. By contrast, the act of giving, no matter how little, activates a flow of money.

I've learnt a lot from one of my stepdaughters about giving to others even when we don't have much money. She's always been incredibly generous with those around her including those she doesn't know. Recently a bus driver let her on the bus for free and rather than spending what she saved on herself, she decided to give it to a homeless person she saw when she got off the bus. This wasn't a one-off act of kindness; she's got a huge heart and regularly helps or gives to those in need. In caring and being this way she naturally attracts opportunities that pass others by.

Reality #01: You can start supporting social causes from the moment you set up in business.

MISCONCEPTION #02: KEEPING THINGS SEPARATE: 'I need to keep my personal giving and business activities separate'

But why?

According to whom?

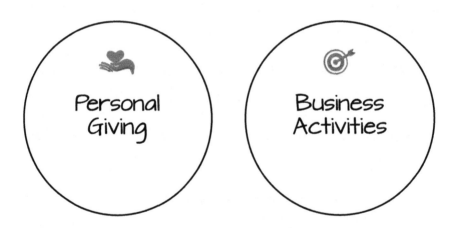

By keeping giving and business activities separate as shown in the above diagram, most business owners are missing out on a great opportunity to grow their business by being kind – simply because they don't know how to do otherwise. However, when you bring these two parts of you together you'll touch the lives of more people.

I'm not advocating only supporting charities through your business – in the course of life you're bound to want

> *You can support social causes through your business without being a registered charity or social enterprise.*

to support social causes personally too. What I'm talking about is proactively also choosing to support social causes through your business.

Reality #02: You can support social causes through your business without being a registered charity or social enterprise.

MISCONCEPTION #03: NO TIME: 'I don't have the time'

This is a common misconception but the reality is that when you incorporate charitable giving into what you already do in the course of your business, it can actually save you time!

One of my great friends Kim is the perfect example of someone who used to think this way but now, like me, uses strategic fundraising as one of her marketing strategies.

In 2007 Kim tragically lost her beloved twelve-year-old son Calum to meningitis. As I'm sure you can imagine this shattered her and her family to the core. However, they've also shown remarkable resilience in the way they have coped with their grief. One of the things that helped Kim through this terrible time was raising funds for a charity called Meningitis Now. Over the years Kim and her family have raised over £60,000, she's set up and run happiness clubs, and published a book called From Heartbreak to Happiness. Kim's husband Sinclair started to publish crime novels in honour of Calum's life and between them they've sold over 130,000 books. They now have a successful accidental business helping others to self-publish books.

Calum would have been twenty-one in 2015, and they were keen to celebrate his life by raising more money for Meningitis Now. But their business had taken off they weren't sure how they could free up the time to do fundraising too. When we first spoke about this Kim felt she had to choose between fundraising and their business because, in her mind, these were two separate activities that both took up a lot of time. So we went through the steps I describe in this book, and they came up with the brilliant idea of the Calum Macleod Memorial Publishing Prize. A competition where the winner would get their book published at no cost. Entrants made a financial donation and submitted the first chapter of their book. By doing this, they raised the funds they wanted for Meningitis Now and had a pipeline of leads that continued to generate sales over the next few months – as a direct consequence of this fundraising competition.

Supporting social causes through your business could help you have more social impact without taking up any extra time.

Remember, this was extra income on the back of fundraising they wanted to do anyway! Had Kim and Sinclair not brought fundraising into the scope of their business, they might not have raised as much money as they did. And they certainly wouldn't have generated the extra income, or list of people wanting to work with them.

Kim says that the main reason the competition worked so well was because the charitable component got them media coverage. This extra visibility helped people hear about them and increased their credibility as experts in the self-publishing world. They also found that the charitable component helped people connect to them and trust them more quickly than other marketing strategies – their story and experience was the same as before, but people seemed to perceive them as more likeable and caring business experts because they liked the authenticity of their fundraising.

What an amazing legacy for Calum – thousands of books being published, and lives touched, because his parents chose to honour and remember his life in this way. It was such a positive experience that Kim and Sinclair now intend to run the competition annually and are already planning prizes for different genres including a 'young writers' award. Calum may not still be in this physical realm, but he is still touching the lives of others around the world.

Reality #03: Supporting social causes through your business could help you have more social impact without taking up any extra time.

MISCONCEPTION #04: WHICH CAUSE?: 'I don't know what cause to support'

This is the second most common block people speak to me about. If you already know what charity or social cause you'd like to support that's great. But if not, don't worry, you don't need one before you start.

Don't let the lack of a cause close to your heart hold you back! Either set aside the money to donate later, or implement what I present in this book.

How to choose a cause to support is discussed in Chapter 9, and as you'll discover in Chapter 3 there are plenty of ways to have social impact without having a particular cause in mind.

I have a friend who, since first setting up in business, knew she wanted to support social causes. But for one reason or another (including being really busy running a profitable business) she's not got round to choosing a cause to support. Rather than let this deter her, she set up a separate bank account she pays money into for this purpose, knowing that one day she'll find the right cause to support.

Reality #04: Don't let the lack of a cause close to your heart hold you back! Either set aside the money to donate later, or implement what I present in this book.

The Give-to-Profit Model

As you can see from the diagram above, the Give-to-Profit model brings together business activities and charitable giving, rather than keeping them separate.

The scope of this includes many different ways to support social causes as discussed in Chapter 3. These include:

- Donations – of money, goods and resources.

- Volunteering your time – using your specialist skills or simply helping out with whatever needs doing.

- Social sourcing – buying business products and services from social suppliers or projects.

- Cause marketing – raising funds for causes with promotional sales campaigns (see Chapter 4 for ideas).

- Sponsorship – of charitable events, projects, people or causes.

A form of 'Corporate Social Responsibility' for small businesses?

A fairer society and a more sustainable future can only be achieved through the practical action of business.
STEPHEN HOWARD, CHIEF EXECUTIVE, BUSINESS IN THE COMMUNITY,[2]

The concept of commercial businesses contributing towards positive social impact is not new. Businesses around the globe have adopted this approach for centuries. Over the last few decades, an increasing number of large organisations have embraced an initiative known as Corporate Social Responsibility (CSR) – conducting their business in ways that are ethical and have a positive impact on society and the environment. However, in large organisations it's not easy to have everyone adopt the same values. Some commercial businesses (such as Virgin, Innocent Drinks and Toms Shoes) do this better than others, as they put social impact at the heart of business strategies, and make socially conscious decisions across their business activities. But in many large organisations, genuine attempts at having positive social impact are only embraced by a few, and can be perceived as a tick-box exercise.

In 1982, Business in the Community (BIC) was founded in the UK as a charitable business network. Under the presidency of The Prince of Wales, BIC brings together businesses to tackle a range of issues with a view to building a fairer and more sustainable society. A similar business network, Business for Social Responsibility, was set up in the US in 1992, followed by CSR Europe in 1996. In the same decade,

2 - *CSR Index Report 2015*

John Elkington published Cannibals with Forks that discussed the need for 21st Century businesses to measure their 'triple bottom line' – their business success in relation to people, planet and profit.

While the scope of supporting social causes in isolation isn't as broad as having a CSR policy, it can certainly form part of a values or impact mission for your business.

To some extent, implementing meaningful social impact strategies can be easier for small businesses than large organisations. We may not have the same resources available but as business owners, we are in the unique position of being able to choose which social causes to support and the scope of activities we'd like to participate in. This can quickly become part of our story and brand (what people think and say about us), which ultimately determines whether they become a client, advocate, partner, supplier, etc.

The Seven Steps to growing a business by supporting charities and social causes

Obviously how you support charities and social causes determines whether your business will grow as a consequence of doing this. I've found that you'll have the greatest positive impact, and return on your investment, when you embrace these seven steps, in this particular order:

1. **Get clear on your 'why'** – the reasons you want to support social causes through your business, including the specific outcomes you'd like for you, your business, and the type of impact you'd like to have.

2. **Define your charitable goal(s)** – a goal you'll work towards that resonates with what's important to you and the impact

you'd like to have. The critical ingredient for growing your business by supporting social causes is to link your charitable and business goals strategically; so both your business and chosen cause benefit.

3. **Choose a cause to support** – if you want to align your business to a cause, select one that touches your heart, satisfies personal needs and is doing good in the world. It's also obviously important to pick one that is reliable, shares your values and is effective in its work.

4. **Come up with compelling ideas** – creative ways to meet your goals that appeal to your audience, and make best use of all available resources.

5. **Optimise your impact** – expand your ideas through the powerful filters of a 'Seven-Plus-Win' model for optimal impact, as described in Chapter 11.

6. **Measure your impact** – identify ways to measure your results and impact so that you know the difference you are actually making and have meaningful information you can share with others.

7. **Share your story** – many customers and businesses nowadays prefer to buy from those who care about social impact so it's becoming increasingly important that you share your story. This is also a great way to raise the visibility of your brand and the cause(s) you support.

These seven steps are important factors to consider no matter how you intend to support social causes. You will find out more in Part 3 of this book.

There is, however, more to your success than knowing what to do. Your mind-set, attitude and how you connect with those you interact with also greatly influences the results you will get.

At the heart of Give-to-Profit

I aim to live my life with love, kindness and compassion in my heart. It's also the approach I take towards business and encourage others to take too. To ignore these pure, powerful and natural human qualities, detaches us from the essence of being human, and what's important in life. In business, adopting a heart-centered approach helps us attract and connect with people who are the best clients, partners, suppliers and collaborators for us.

To me, if we all acted more often from a place of love, rather than fear or greed (common destructive driving forces), the world would be a very different place. I share more about this and how to put yourself in the best place for experiencing happiness and success in my book *Heartatude: The 9 Principles of Heart-Centered Success*. In summary these are:

1. Engage your heart

2. Make a difference

3. Be the masterful authentic leader you were born to be

4. Take personal responsibility

5. Manage your emotions

6. Embrace possibility and success

7. Act consciously with positive intention

8. Develop meaningful connections and relationships

9. Tap into natural energy sources for peak performance.

In practical terms there are three keys at the heart of the Give-to-Profit model:

Love – always act from a place of love, kindness and compassion in your heart, towards yourself as much as others. While there are times when it's advisable to be strategic about deciding what to do, let your heart determine how you act. Yes that's right, there is a place for LOVE in business!

Impact – focus on how to have the greatest positive impact while also keeping what you do simple. Be strategic and leverage your time, money and resources (and those of others), so you can give generously to others in a way that's also kind to you. This includes evaluating, monitoring and sharing your social impact, for example being transparent about the amounts raised, number of people helped get out of poverty, houses you've built or items donated.

Balance – between giving to yourself and giving to others; of giving and receiving; having a good balance between your personal life and business; charging fair market prices; making conscious decisions about when to charge versus offering your services for free or for charitable donations; unconditional giving in the moment and strategic giving in what you offer through your product/service range; listening to your head and your heart; setting intentions while at the same time being unattached to outcomes.

Is Give-to-Profit the right business model for you?

While connecting your commercial business to a charitable cause can be a great way to grow your business, it isn't the right way forward for everyone. I have friends who have set up registered charities, foundations and social enterprises because doing so was a better way to manifest their vision. Others I know own a commercial business that supports a charitable entity they also set up – adopting a similar model to what I suggest in this book, though supporting a social cause they also run.

Of course a huge benefit of registering a formal social enterprise, charity or foundation is that you may be eligible to apply for charitable grants and funding. But these are not suitable models for many business ventures.

If you don't want to set up a formal charitable entity or are unsure about committing to this yet, the Give-to-Profit model is a flexible and legitimate way to still have a social impact through your business. As you'll also discover, there are sometimes ways you can still benefit from 'social' funding even if you're not a registered charity or social cause.

Key Points

- You can have a social mission to your business without needing to be a registered charity, foundation or social enterprise.

- You don't have to wait until you have the money to support a charity or social cause – supporting a social cause can actually help you grow your business, client base and income.

- By incorporating charitable activities into your business you can save yourself time and money while at the same time help more people.

- There are many ways to support social causes, other than making financial donations.

❤ You don't need to have a cause close to your heart – this book discusses strategies for having social impact without selecting one specific cause to support, and will help you choose one if you want to do so.

❤ Being authentic and acting from a place of love, kindness and compassion is at the heart of the Give-to-Profit model.

 Social Impact Actions

Download the free Give-to-Profit Practical Guide that accompanies this book at www.givetoprofit.com

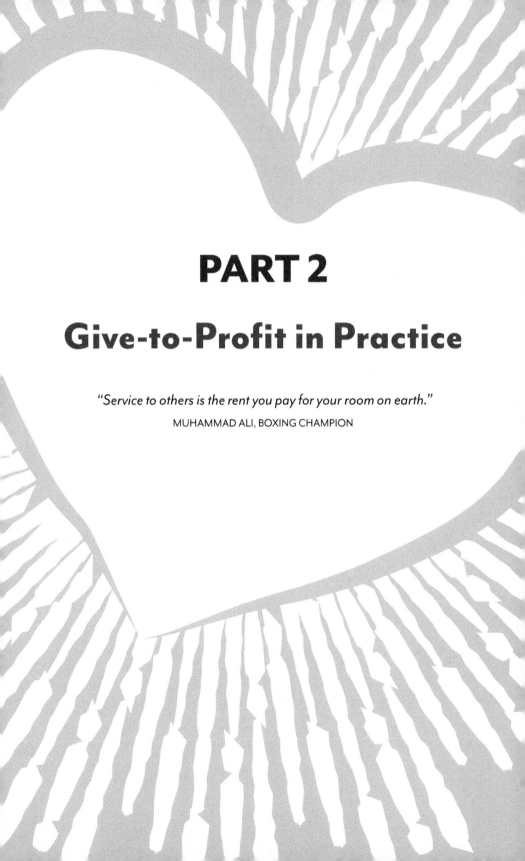

PART 2

Give-to-Profit in Practice

"Service to others is the rent you pay for your room on earth."

MUHAMMAD ALI, BOXING CHAMPION

3

Twenty-Five Ways to Support Charities and Social Causes Through Your Business

*"We can learn to see each other and see ourselves in
each other and recognize that human beings
are more alike than we are unalike."*

MAYA ANGELOU, AUTHOR

So you don't need to wait until you've made a profit to support social causes through your business – there are plenty ways to put social giving at the heart of your business that will help you grow your business, and could even save you money.

For many business owners the most obvious way to do this is by donating a percentage of sales or profits. Yes, most social causes desperately need financial support but there are other ways too – we can help them raise funds, save money and be more effective in their work.

Many studies have shown that giving financial hand-outs may help people in critical moments but they often need more than money.

Over the long-term the traditional model of charity aid and giving financial hand-outs breeds dependency rather than what those on low incomes consistently say they'd prefer: dignified jobs that give regular income they can use to improve their lives and create more sustainable communities. They also often need trauma healing.

If you take the Syrian Refugee Crisis that's gripping Europe as I write, there are so many people affected who need food, drink, clothing and a safe warm place to sleep. Having money in itself isn't going to help unless they also have access to places where they can buy what they need. Reputable charities overseeing relief operations are often better equipped to buy and distribute critical aid, so donating money to them can be the easiest and quickest way to help those on the ground. Donating goods, time, skills and physical space is often also appreciated – not just overseas but also locally too. For example, supporting refugees or participating in relief efforts in your community.

There are endless possible ways to support social causes through business. Here are some strategies to consider:

1. **Donate a percentage of your sales or profits to charity** – calculating the amount you donate based on the value of your sales or profits for any given transaction or time period.

2. **Make ad-hoc financial donation**s – choosing the value and frequency of donations, as and when you want to make them.

3. **Make regular financial donations** – donating regular fixed amounts.

Depending where you live, the way your business is set up, and the legal status of the specific cause you support, you may be able to off-set financial donations against future tax liabilities. Check with your financial adviser to find out whether this could apply to you. It's also worth checking whether the donations you make are considered as corporate philanthropy or fall inside the scope and governance of cause marketing (see Chapter 5).

4. **Donate a product for every product sold** – this is the model used by Toms Shoes where one pair of shoes is donated for every pair of shoes sold. You could donate the same type of product, as Toms Shoes do, or you could donate a completely different product.

5. **Donate resources for every product sold** – here you make a donation of something needed by those you want to help (for example a mosquito net, food to feed a child for a month, or to pay for a child's education) every time a specific product/ service is sold.

    If this strategy is of interest, it's worth checking out the organisation *Buy1GIVE1* that facilitates a way you can easily do this and measure the impact of your giving.

6. **Donate unsold stock** – rather than sitting on old stock or throwing it out, find a cause who would really appreciate it. For example I know of a retailer in the UK who donated unsold toys to a local hospital for sick children.

7. **Invite buyers to make a donation when making a purchase** – at its simplest this may be a charity box at the checkout into which customers can put their spare change (or more). Or you might add an optional donation to your checkout process where customers can add a donation to their purchase while paying; just as they would add a tip. You could

suggest an amount for example £1 or $1 or invite people to choose how much they'd like to give. I've experienced this request from many hotels and more recently online when making an Amazon purchase.

When making donations based on product sales (as per examples five, six and seven above) you can decide whether to apply this across all products/services or to come up with product-specific giving.

8. **Buy social** – one of the easiest ways to have social impact through your business is to buy from 'social' suppliers. In the course of business there are many times when we buy products or services from others. But have you ever considered buying these from social enterprises or charities? If not, you're missing out on a great opportunity to have more positive social impact, at no extra cost. Buying social could even save you money. I cover this further in Chapter 6.

9. **Social outsourcing or hiring** – similar to social sourcing, this is where you employ or contract individuals who have experienced personal challenges (such as poverty, abuse, neglect, war, trauma or life-threatening injury or illness). In other words, having a conscious intention to help those who find it hard to get well-paid jobs, and working out how you can help each other – with you giving them opportunities to work and them providing you with the skills you need.

   Many social enterprises are set up to employ people who have experienced hardship but you don't need to be a social business to do this. Commercial businesses can also add a social element to their recruitment (as long as you also pay attention to any relevant legislation you have in your country or state in relation to equal opportunities). Let's help more people out of poverty!

10. **Fundraising** – this could be fundraising events, charitable sales promotions, or point of sale collections, at your place of work or incorporated into other business activities.

Organising fundraising events has become one of my favourite marketing strategies because fundraising events can be a great way to showcase your expertise, give people a good experience, and raise funds for charity, all at the same time. When you come up with fundraising events your ideal clients find highly attractive, these can fit in really well with other business activities and help you connect better your followers or community. They can also help you expand the reach and effectiveness of other marketing strategies such as social media or joint venture partnerships. There are so many ways to raise funds through your business, see Chapter 4 for ideas.

Please note in many countries there is legislation and regulations that govern raising funds for charity through a business (commonly known as 'cause marketing'). See Chapter 5 for further information about this.

11. **Secure funding to provide products or services to social causes** – and yes, supporting social causes includes earning money from them where appropriate too. Charities and social enterprises pay for products and services in the same way other consumers do. If they are part of your target market, you're hopefully already charging them.

It's worth exploring whether there is any local or national funding to cover the cost of what you provide. Funding that either you or the social cause could apply for. For example, I sit on the board of a social enterprise that helps young people lead happier healthy lives through teaching basic life skills. Some of our projects are delivered through schools who themselves seek the funding from other sources. I've also been paid to deliver training to charities and social enterprises that obtained funding to pay for this.

While there are many foundations that provide funding for social causes, there are also many causes 'competing' for these pots of money. A helpful perspective to have is that trustees of charitable foundations are tasked with finding good causes to allocate their funds to – your project could be the perfect fit. Someone gets the money, why not your project?

I have a friend who runs a profitable business and is a great supporter of social causes both personally and through her business. She raises funds for charity, volunteers her time and is also exploring how she can provide services within prisons – on a paid (funded) basis. It's your business and so you can work out your own perfect mix of paid work versus volunteering.

To explore funding sources I suggest you do an Internet search and ask the causes you'd like to support whether they know of any relevant funding providers. It's also worth speaking to those who are already serving this audience.

12. **Share your time on a voluntary basis** – you could offer the specialist skills you provide commercially through your business, or completely different skills that others need and would be grateful to receive.

For instance, I remember when I first started out in business my primary aim was to earn enough money to live on as a coach and therapist. However, one of the things I'm really good at is strategic thinking and business management of larger enterprises. Early on I found my small business didn't give me the scope to use my brain in this way. That was one of the reasons I decided to become a trustee with a charity. The charity needed people who could help develop their business strategies and I wanted to continue to do that kind of work.

However, you can obviously also volunteer your time and help others in ways other than sharing your specialist skills or knowledge. You could instead approach social causes and do whatever they need help with such as serving refreshments at a homeless shelter, hospice or at community events.

How does volunteering help grow your business? One of the main benefits is that you'll grow your network. I've found that when you work with people on a common cause or mission, these connections often flourish into some of the best relationships we make – both personally, and for our business. Depending on what you do, you could develop new skills or get personal needs met that you're not getting met through your business, for example social interaction if you run a home-based business. Volunteering can also be a great way to boost your emotional well-being, self-esteem and confidence.

In many traditional cultures individuals call upon their family, friends and people in their community to help with difficult tasks or to help them get through challenging times. This still happens around the world especially in rural communities. Sadly there are likely to be plenty people feeling alone, isolated and in need of help in your community.

After the 1994 Rwandan genocide, the country introduced monthly community service days (known as Umuganda) that require all Rwandans to work on community projects, to help rebuild the country. On these days nothing much else happens other than the provision of critical basic services. In the context of business, Taiwan operates a similar policy for all workers – having specific days of the year when everyone undertakes charitable work. While there are some who don't agree with compulsory nature of these practices in Rwanda and Taiwan, there are so many benefits of doing unpaid work in the community – particularly if you choose to do it!

How much time you donate is up to you. You can commit to a project for an agreed time, help others on an ad-hoc basis or join the micro-volunteering movement – people doing good in short bursts of time from only ten minutes at a time. Micro-volunteering is something you can do from home without even getting dressed!

There are details of a couple of organisations you can use to find volunteering opportunities on my website at www. givetoprofit.com. And of course it's also worth connecting with social causes in your local community as well as doing your own Internet search.

13. **Support others' charitable events** – there are many people organising charitable events which you could support such as by donating gifts for raffles or auctions, raising funds,

helping out, sponsoring the event or taking a table, or promoting it the event itself.

14. **Become an ambassador or advocate for a cause** – telling others about a cause's work and how they can help. Recently someone at one of my networking events mentioned a charity she was doing some work for who were looking for smart clothing to be donated to attendees of one of their programmes, one that helps women into the workplace including equipping them with clothes to wear to interviews and their new jobs.

15. **Give personal introductions** – an easy act of kindness that could transform the fortune of social causes is to introduce them to people in your personal or business network.

    When you meet people from charities and social causes, ask them what they need or who they'd like to be introduced to, be it funders, suppliers, business partners, agents or celebrities. Then take the time to review your business contacts to see if there is anyone you could introduce them to. Connecting people to one another is one of the greatest gifts you can give.

16. **Give social causes access to business resources** – when you provide resources to social causes you are helping them save money. Examples of resources you could offer include physical space, equipment, people (in terms of hours or skills) or technology. If you employ staff or work collaboratively with others, think of ways you do this as a team building or staff engagement activity.

17. **Sponsor a specific person who needs support** – perhaps paying for a young child to attend school (with or without

uniform and materials) or for a young person to complete higher education (with or without their living costs). This is a really easy and measurable way to have social impact through your business, especially if you go through a registered charity that has already worked out the costs and logistics of converting donations into the form of support needed by the beneficiaries.

Once you've identified a cause you'd like to support (see Chapter 9), you can find out suggested one-off, monthly or annual donations. You can then decide how to cover this – whether this be donating the funds from your business profits, or raising funds for this specific purpose.

Sometimes charities ask supporters to provide certain items to individuals (fully or in part). In the case of the charity I go to Rwanda with, we have sponsors who donate university fees, computers, and other specific resources that are needed on an ongoing basis.

18. **Sponsoring charitable projects** – in a similar way to sponsoring a person, you could sponsor a charitable project, by covering the costs or providing resources. Again, fully or in part. I recently ran an online training event with the specific intention of raising enough money to build a home for a family in Malawi. Attendees made financial donations to attend; I delivered the training and forwarded the funds to the young people building the house. Four weeks later a widow and her disabled toddler moved into their new home – thanks to the generosity of my business community.

19. **Sponsoring events** – there are many ways to sponsor events such as taking a stand or table, advertising in a programme,

offering samples, tasters or other resources (for example donating raffle prizes or gifts for goodie bags). You could sponsor a whole event or just part of it.

20. **Sponsoring the purchase of specific resources** – charitable causes often ask people and businesses to donate particular items needed by those they help, e.g. tents, mosquito nets, football strips, computers, vaccinations, books, educational costs, etc. I'm involved in a social enterprise called Lead a Bright Future where we sell products to help prevent bullying in schools and communities. One of the things we invite our supporters to do is to buy a Buddy Bear Friend Backpack (full of resources to tackle bullying) that we can give to schools that are committed to helping young children feel better about themselves, and support others in their school.

    By sponsoring the purchase of specific resources you're effectively donating what's needed, without needing to worry about buying and distributing the goods yourself.

21. **Pay-it-Forward Campaigns** – if you've seen the film or read the book Pay-It-Forward you'll know what this is about. If this is the first time you've heard the phrase, the book and film are worth checking out! Pay-it-forward is about being kind or generous to someone without any expectation of payment, and with the request that the beneficiary 'pays' by doing something kind for someone else.

    Ways you could do this through your business include:

    • Asking your customers to buy an extra one of what they are buying for themselves, to give to someone else, e.g. to buy an extra coffee to give to a homeless person.

- Offering your time or expertise to someone on the basis they 'pay-it-forward' by helping someone else.

- Giving a product or service to someone who can't afford to pay for it, if they agree to 'pay-it-forward'.

22. **Selectively offer your products and services for free** – have a policy for scholarships, pro-bono work for those who can't afford to pay for your services. Or create give-away events. I was inspired to see a local sandwich shop open its doors on Christmas Day to serve free meals to the homeless.

23. **Collaborate with social causes** – collaboration is a powerful way to grow most businesses. Rather than only partnering with other businesses, how about considering how you could also collaborate with social causes?

24. **Social lending** – lending money to social causes, either directly or through firms set up to facilitate this. Rather than donating funds, an arrangement is put in place for the cause to pay you back the money. There are many micro-finance schemes that enable you do this with social causes around the world.

25. **Social investment** – similar to social lending in that the intention is that you can get your money back but rather than lending the cause the money, you own a share of the cause or social enterprise.

Key Points

- There are many ways you can support charities and social causes, with various levels of commitment in terms of time, money and resources.

- You don't have to wait until you've generated money or profits to do this – there are ways to put charitable giving at the heart of your business that could have immediate social impact, save money and grow your business.

- The best strategies for you depend on why supporting social causes is important to you, the resources you have available and the difference you'd like to make in the world.

Which of the ways I've suggested appeal to you the most?

What other ideas do you have?

Resources

Check out the next three chapters for fundraising ideas, cause marketing and further information on social buying.

If you'd like further information about how to find volunteering or social investment opportunities I've listed some useful websites and resources on my website www.givetoprofit.com.

Fifty-Two Ways to Raise Funds for Causes Through Your Business

"The goal of a non-profit seeking money needs to be to create an environment in which the community congratulates itself on overpaying.

SETH GODIN, AUTHOR and THOUGHT LEADER

Raising funds for social causes can be a fun and effective way to grow your business if you link your fundraising activities to your business strategically. I explain how to do this in Chapters 8 and 10.

Here I list some fundraising ideas I've seen and used as others have told me they find hearing these helpful ahead of coming up with their own ideas. Before committing to any fundraising activities, remember to check out whether they are governed by legislation such as that relating to cause marketing or selling raffle tickets, and if there are any tax implications for you (or the cause you're supporting) to consider and manage. Here are some ideas to get you started:

At point of sale

1. Offer fundraising products at the checkout – have small impulse-buy products customers can easily add to their purchase.

2. Invite people to make a donation at the checkout – you may have experienced this when checking out at hotels or when making purchases on Amazon.

3. Have a donation box – at your checkout, reception area, trade shows, events, etc.

In-person marketing

4. Hold a charitable fundraising event that is attractive to your ideal clients, e.g. a training, taster, talent contest, client entertainment or social event.

5. Set up a meet-up group for regular networking or mentoring events for which you 'charge' an entry fee donation.

6. Run a regular business network and donate all or a percentage of profits to charity.

7. Collaborate with others in your network to come up with a fundraising event that showcases all your talents.

8. Ask organisers of other networks if you can 'sell' your fundraising products at their events.

9. Ask network organisers if you can do a talk about your fundraising project and/or sell fundraising products at their events.

10. Rather than speaking for free, ask event organisers to make a donation to your social cause and/or for you to have the opportunity to sell your fundraising products or services.

11. Invite others in your network to help you raise funds by selling your fundraising products to people they know – either on behalf of your chosen cause or one they're supporting.

12. Take a table at a charity fundraising event and invite key people you'd like to network with to attend.

At in-person events (e.g. conferences, client entertainment or networking events)

13. Hold a raffle – with prizes likely to appeal to your audience (donated by you and your contacts).

14. Invite attendees to bring along a raffle prize and then sell raffle tickets and hold the raffle at the event. You could also combine this with pre-attendance online raffle sales.

15. Ask speakers to donate high value products, gifts, or experiences in advance and take bids from your audience during the event.

16. Invite attendees to bring along a certain item that you could collect and sell for charity, e.g. CDs, old mobile phones, DVDs, pieces of gold or silver.

17. Invite someone who has benefited from your charitable work to speak at one of your events – and then invite donations from the audience.

18. Invite someone from the cause(s) you're supporting to speak at your event – and then invite donations from the audience. You could also offer to match donations up to a certain amount.

19. Create an activity that gets your audience involved in the fundraising, e.g. getting them to come up with ways that they could help you raise funds or to come up with ways they could raise £100 to donate to your cause.

20. Create a challenge or activity that gives your brand and chosen cause more visibility. For example, Innocent Drinks invites people around the UK to knit small hats to go on their bottled drinks, and donates money to a cause for every bottle with a hat sold.

21. Create an audience resourcefulness challenge, e.g. a commitment to raise £100.

22. Run a fundraising activity helping your audience to come up with ways to save a small amount each month, e.g. £10. Then ask if they would be willing to now donate £5 of that a month to your cause or a cause of their choice? Get them to share their pledges.

23. Ask partners at your event(s) if they will donate a percentage or all their share of profits from that event to a cause (chosen by either of you).

24. When selling products at events, give buyers a token for every £10 they spend and ask them to select which of three causes they'd like you to make a donation to. You could

even ask your audience to help come up with the shortlist of causes as an engagement strategy, before or during the event.

Online fundraising events

25. Hold an online auction – with products and services donated from those in your community. You can invite applications for donors if you want to manage what you offer.

26. Run an online raffle – again using products and services donated by people in your community.

27. Run a fundraising interview series your audience would love and be happy to pay for (e.g. one event a month for £10/US$15).

28. Run a fundraising tele-summit – e.g. with 50% of profits going to your desired charity and the other 50% going to charities chosen by the speakers.

29. Bundle online products, interviews and resources into online fundraising packages.

30. Run an online competition – e.g. asking attendees to raise as much as they can for charity over a month, and offer a compelling prize or donation to the person who raises the most.

When marketing online products

31. Run a fundraising 'taster' webinar – instead of a 'giveaway' event, taster or free webinar, turn these into fundraising

events by charging a nominal amount and donating proceeds or profits to charity. These could be training, networking, discussion, party or interviews, etc.

32. When working with business partners, let them know you're donating a percentage of sales to a social cause and ask if they'd be interested in doing the same.

33. Let people know that with every purchase you'll be donating a specified amount or goods to charity (e.g. to buy two mosquito nets) – assuming there is the profit margin in your pricing to do this.

34. Offer 'fundraising' products as bonuses when selling online products and give an amount to charity for each product included. When others supply these I like to make a donation to a cause of their choice.

Business-related projects

35. Donate all sales proceeds during a specified day(s) to charity. For example the outdoor retailer Patagonia donated 100% of its Black Friday global sales, totalling US$10 million to charities in 2016 – five times its anticipated sales for the day.

36. Create a fundraising product you can sell for charity indefinitely.

37. Instead of deciding to stop selling 'old' stock you could re-package it as a fundraising product(s).

38. Write an e-book or record a business audio – give all sales proceeds to charity.

39. Offer fundraising house parties – sharing your knowledge and selling fundraising products.

40. Instead of doing free pilots, run them as fundraising events – inviting donations from attendees.

41. Team building/staff engagement activities – explore the potential to incorporate fundraising or social impact projects into these activities. For example the social enterprise *WildHearts* offers a scheme called Micro-Tyco that offers a team building challenge to businesses around the world whereby teams have a month to turn £1 into as much money as possible whilst receiving world-class business training, endorsed by Babson College. *WildHearts* then invests the funds raised in micro loans for poor entrepreneurs in the developing world.

42. Have those from the cause you're supporting create a product that you can sell at your events, when networking or to your database.

43. If the cause you're supporting has a large audience of your ideal clients as its supporters, offer to deliver a fundraising event to their supporters.

44. If the cause has a large audience of your ideal clients, set them up as an affiliate for your products, e.g. paying them 50% of any referral revenue. And help them 'sell' these to their supporters.

45. Come up with a referral incentive scheme for your clients – one that rewards your clients and raises funds for charity, every time they refer a client to you.

46. Giving gift cards – as well as offering gift vouchers for your products or services you could offer charitable gifts vouchers whereby you make a donation when these are purchased, and the person buying gets a card or voucher they can give as a gift to someone else.

47. If you run a business network or meet-up group, invite members of the group to come up with and organise a fundraiser together.

48. Ask the charity or cause you're supporting how they think you could raise funds for them.

Non-business-related projects you could offer to your audience

49. Use one of your other talents to create a highly consumable product you can sell at networking events, that makes you more memorable, and raises funds for charity.

50. Record a song or short film and give all sales proceeds to charity.

51. Become a distributor for a high quality 'multi-level marketing' product and donate all sales proceeds from this to charity.

52. Become an eBay trader selling certain items on behalf of your community/business network and give all proceeds to your chosen cause.

These are just some of the things I've done or seen others doing. I'm sure there are many more ways you could raise funds for social causes through your business – especially as more businesses embrace the concept of charitable giving and advances in technology present new opportunities.

What ideas appeal most to you?

Key Points

- ❤ There is a multitude of ways to raise funds for charity through your business.

- ❤ Remember, in many countries there is legislation that governs activities that are classified as 'cause' marketing. You can find out more about this in the next chapter.

5

Cause Marketing – Definition, Best Practices and Legislation

"Cause marketing is a partnership between a non-profit and for-profit for mutual profit."

JOE WATERS – AUTHOR, SPEAKER and PODCAST HOST

The world of business-giving is evolving and changing at a rapid pace.

Supporting charities through your business can be a powerful way to make a difference, both locally and further afield. But if you're thinking of any kind of charitable sales promotion there could be legal and tax implications to consider first. As more and more companies introduce new ways to support social causes, there's increasing pressure for 'cause marketing' to be regulated – to protect consumers and ensure businesses and non-profits apply best practices.

Even simply mentioning that you donate a percentage of sales to charity in your marketing could be a notifiable act in some parts of the world. That said, while cause marketing legislation is a factor to consider before deciding which charitable activities to do through your business, it is far less onerous than setting up a charity, non-profit, foundation or social enterprise. It's also a small cost to pay relative to the challenges those you want to help are likely to experience every day.

The purpose of this chapter is twofold: the first half aims to clarify what is meant by 'cause marketing' and to highlight potentially exempt activities so you can decide what would suit you and your business; while the second half gives you practical advice on how to approach fundraising campaigns and negotiate any legislative hurdles.

The information in this chapter is intended to give you a few pointers so you can operate your charitable activities within the law. However, please be aware that I am not a lawyer, that legislation is different around the world, and is constantly changing. It is therefore important to check out relevant legislation that might apply to you. You will find some useful resources to help you do this on my website www. givetoprofit.com.

Which fundraising activities are regulated?

This very much depends on what you do, where your business is located, the scope of your fundraising (e.g. local, national or international), the type of cause you support, and whether it's you, or your business, that is supporting the cause.

Much of this chapter may not apply if you plan to support a social cause in a way that doesn't involve fundraising, for example volunteering your time, donating resources (such as computers, food or clothing), or making philanthropic financial donations (of money that's not been generated by charitable sales promotions).

That said, since there are potential legal, regulatory and tax implications to consider, and because the definition of 'cause marketing' differs around the world, I'd still suggest reading what I discuss here, so you can make informed decisions, and get appropriate advice, to ensure you comply with any relevant laws. Even if what you decide to do isn't governed by cause marketing legislation, you could still adopt some of the best practices I suggest.

The legal framework

Charities themselves are encouraged to monitor all fundraising activities conducted for their benefit, whether they are a passive or active participator. There are also potential legal, regulatory and tax implications for charities, e.g. if they promote you, they may need to pay tax on your 'donations'.

I've found that having a basic understanding of the legal, regulatory and tax frameworks has helped me decide which charitable activities to get involved in and when to raise funds personally versus through my business.

At the time of writing this book, cause marketing is a regulated activity in at least twenty US States. This means that if you operate your business in one of these, there are things you need to do before, during, and after any kind of charitable sales promotion.

In the UK, when you raise funds for a registered charity through your business, your actions are regulated by several laws including those which require businesses to have an agreement in place with charities they raise funds for, before undertaking any charitable sales promotions. At the time of writing, charitable sales campaigns in favour of social enterprises, B-Corps, and 'unofficial' causes in the UK are not governed by cause marketing legislation.

Legislation also governs fundraising activities in Europe, Canada and Australia where cause marketing is becoming more popular.

Of course the usual business advertising standards apply to all marketing and sales campaigns.

What is cause marketing?

Cause marketing relates to activities where a commercial business runs a charitable sales promotion or marketing campaign, for mutual financial benefit – for them and the cause. Other names for cause marketing include commercial co-ventures in the US, or commercial participators in the UK.

At a deeper level, cause marketing is all about appealing to the emotions of your audience, connecting with them, and giving them the opportunity to feel part of something good when they buy from you. Remember, Millennials are a generation that favours socially conscious businesses.

Examples of potential cause marketing activities include:

- A business donating a proportion of sales proceeds to a charity, and mentioning this in their marketing.

- A business organising a fundraising event for, or in aid of, a charity.

- A business inviting buyers to make a donation to a selected charity, when they pay for products or services.

- Action-triggered donations – where a company makes a donation when others take specific action, e.g. buy a product, or share/like a social media post.

- A charity promoting your products or services to their audience, e.g. by email or social media.

Please note that in some countries (or states) cause marketing applies:

- Whenever a business promises to support a cause – the cause doesn't need to be named.

- Even if a sale doesn't take place – the legislation is activated by simply naming a charity.

Phrases such as cause marketing, strategic philanthropy, corporate philanthropy, strategic giving, and commercial co-ventures are sometimes interpreted and used interchangeably, as though they all mean the same thing. But they don't.

This matters because different laws apply to each. Only once you understand the subtle differences can you make informed decisions and comply with relevant laws. With this in mind I thought I'd share some useful distinctions, so you can determine whether your social giving activities are subject to 'cause marketing' legislation. Or not.

Cause marketing versus sponsorship

A distinction I've found helpful is that cause marketing is where a charity allows its name or brand to be associated with business activities. For example, Innocent Drinks donates 10% of profits to charity, with the majority going to their charitable foundation. Since 2003 they have also raised money for Age UK through the Innocent Big Knit I mentioned earlier.

Whereas sponsorship is the opposite in that the business pays to have its name associated with a charity's activities. For example, Virgin Money sponsor the London Marathon, which is organised by a charitable foundation.

Cause marketing versus strategic philanthropy

Strategic or corporate philanthropy is where a commercial business makes donations to charitable causes, without any expectation of commercial gain, or goodwill. If consumers are not specifically asked to take action to trigger any giving, e.g. where your business makes financial donations to charitable causes, but you don't mention this in your marketing literature or campaigns, this is usually considered corporate philanthropy rather than cause marketing.

Cause marketing versus corporate social responsibility

Corporate social responsibility (CSR) is 'the voluntary action businesses take over and above legal requirements to manage and enhance economic, environmental and societal impacts'.[3] CSR has a far wider scope than supporting charities or social causes as it includes the conscious impact businesses aim to have on communities (e.g. in terms of infrastructure, supporting community projects), the environment (e.g. disposal of waste, materials or energy used) and the lives of people (their employees, customers and those in the communities they operate). However, as part of a wider CSR strategy an organisation may decide to participate in charitable sales promotions or fundraising activities.

Large organisations often have committees which organise charitable activities, e.g. helping out with charitable projects, donating Easter Eggs or fundraising through cake sales or dress-down days. Most of these are unlikely to be considered 'cause marketing' unless their customers are asked to participate or what they are doing is used in their marketing.

3 - *Corporate Responsibility Report produced by The Department for Business Innovation & Skills, UK Government, June 2014, p3.*

Cause marketing is not the same as sponsorship or strategic philanthropy. However, some corporate social responsibility activities could be classified as cause marketing.

Cause marketing versus social investment

Social investment is where you lend to or invest money in a social cause. You can do this either as an individual or through your business. With social investment you are not donating or giving your money to the social cause. You are lending or investing your money, with the expectation you will get it back. Obviously there is a risk you won't, but you can reduce risk by investing money through a micro-finance organisation or an investment company. The act of investing in or lending to social causes is not cause marketing. However, if you raised the funds through an activity that would be classified as cause marketing, then relevant laws and governance would apply to that campaign.

Cause marketing best practices

The following best practices are guiding principles designed to help you navigate your way through the cause marketing maze, whether or not your charitable activities are subject to any specific laws or regulations. Implementing these will give you, the cause and consumers more clarity about the scope of your charitable activities:

1. Comply with the law

    Find out what laws apply to the type of activity that you want to do and apply these. Obviously this involves getting appropriate advice from qualified advisers. Useful links to help you find out more are on my website at www.givetoprofit.com.

2. Put a formal agreement in place

    Before you start your cause marketing campaign, put a formal agreement in place to clarify key information, responsibilities, practicalities and timeframes for both parties.

    The basic information to state includes: all the parties involved (names and addresses); date the agreement was signed; how donations will be calculated; the information to be disclosed to consumers in marketing communications (see the following points); how you can use the charity's logo; the practicalities of the campaign; when and how you will make payments; how you'll account for or demonstrate relevant sales; duration of agreement; and terms relating to amendments or early termination.

    You may also want to include information on how you'll monitor and report your fundraising, before, during and after your charitable campaign.

    Some charities will have legal contracts they use with their supporters so it's worth asking them if they have one.

3. File and register your charitable sales campaign (where required)

    It is important to remember what you need to comply with is governed by the type of cause you are supporting, where you operate as a business, and the geographic reach of your charitable sales campaign.

    In some countries and states you need to do more than have an agreement in place before launching a charitable sales campaign.

If you are in the US you may also need to file and register your campaign in your state, and for national campaigns across all states concerned.

At the time of writing, there is not the same requirement to register cause-marketing campaigns in the UK.

When it comes to global and online campaigns, legislation has still to catch up around the world. For international or on-line charitable sales campaigns I suggest you adhere to the laws that apply in the country(s) or state(s) your business operates, and take advice on whether you need to do more.

4. Be transparent to consumers

    Avoid any vague and misleading statements, and disclose the following in your marketing:

- The specific cause(s) that's going to benefit from this campaign or event, including any specific purpose for the money, e.g. to build a house or fund the purchase of certain goods.

- If more than one charity is going to benefit, what proportion will go to each.

- The monetary amount (or item) that will be donated for each purchase rather than only stating a percentage of profits/sales.

In some countries you must state the actual amount you'll be donating (e.g. £1.50 for every product sold, or, at least, to state the estimated amount (number of items) to be donated per sale.

- The minimum and maximum agreed contribution (e.g. up to £10,000, or up to twenty bikes).

- The duration of your fundraising campaign.

Have the above information easily visible to consumers on packaging or at the point of sale, so it's easy for them to understand all key facts, before deciding whether to buy from you or not.

Other ways to be transparent include:

- Evaluating your efforts, and reporting these to your chosen cause, and publically to consumers, e.g. on your website or in your business premises.

- Applying the same levels of transparency with both online and offline campaigns.

- Keep your campaign or fundraising simple – so consumers can easily understand exactly what they'll be supporting by making a purchase.

5. Distribute charitable proceeds promptly

    Some countries state required payment time-frames. Otherwise, agree with the cause you're supporting when you'll forward funds, e.g. within 30 days of the end of the campaign.

6. Maintain accurate records

    Keep accurate records of sales, donations and campaigns.

7. Help charitable causes comply with the law

    There are potential legal, regulatory and tax implications for those you are raising funds for, depending on the extent to which they get involved in your campaign. Many larger organisations will know what to do and will have procedures and processes in place that will help. However, you may need to guide smaller organisations into getting the relevant advice.

If you live in the US, I suggest you check out *The Ten Commandments of Cause Marketing Law written by Karen I Wu* – you can find out more about these at www.givetoprofit.com.

How to avoid cause-marketing legislation

Obviously if what you do is considered cause marketing in the jurisdictions of your charitable sales campaign, you need to take account of the relevant laws.

However, there are plenty ways to support social causes and donate money to them that are not classified as cause-marketing activities:

- Support causes not regulated by cause-marketing legislation (while still applying best practices).

- Support social causes in ways other than raising funds for them – I shared ideas for this in Chapter 3.

- Donate funds without mentioning this in your marketing – this is philanthropy.

- Sponsor a charity's events or operations – with a supporting sponsorship agreement.

- Support an unrecognised social cause – e.g. a First Giving Campaign set up by an individual or someone you know who needs help due to personal illness or tragedy.

- Support social causes personally.

Just like any other individual, business owners can raise funds for charity personally – we don't have to do our charitable fundraising through our business.

If you are a solo-preneur, you and your business are often perceived as one. In other words, your personal and business brands are not distinct but interlinked. What people think about your business is greatly influenced by what you do personally – both the good and bad. This is similar to the way that the personal actions of high-profile politicians, celebrities, or business leaders have an impact on how others perceive them in their professional roles.

When you're the owner or figurehead of a small business, supporting charities personally is likely to have a positive impact on your business.

- Does the fact that someone supports social causes influence your opinion of them?

- Are you more likely to buy from people with similar values?

There will be times when it's in everyone's best interests to put your charitable activities through your business. However, there are likely to also be times you want to support charities personally too.

When I go to Rwanda, I do this because I want to personally. The trips themselves are not part of my business and neither is much of the fundraising I do that's associated with that humanitarian work.

I just started making bracelets and earrings to raise funds for my trips and all sorts of people started buying them – they were not designed specifically to appeal to my business audience. Nor were they sold through my business.

Key Points

 Check out what cause marketing legislation applies where you operate your business before doing any fundraising for charities or social causes through your business!

 Irrespective of whether your charitable sales campaigns are considered cause-marketing, it's still prudent to apply best practices. With the rise in social-impact-driven businesses, and consumer trends increasingly favouring companies who put social impact at the heart of their businesses, it's likely that cause -marketing regulations will increase.

 Cause marketing legislation may be an extra hurdle to navigate, but please don't let this put you off. Setting up a business with a social mission is much easier than setting up a registered charity, foundation, or social enterprise.

 If you don't want to have to get your head around cause-marketing legislation, there are plenty other ways you can support social causes as described in Chapter 3.

Social Impact Actions

If you'd like further information about what applies to your charitable sales promotions or cause marketing legislation, I've listed several useful websites and resources on my website www.givetoprofit.com.

6

Buying Social

"When you hire people who've never had a chance before, who've never had the ability to have formal employment, they take their jobs extremely seriously."

LEILA JANAH, FOUNDER of SAMASOURCE

One of the easiest ways to have social impact through your business is to buy from 'social' suppliers. By doing this you can make a difference in the world without spending any extra money, time or resources. It's a subtle yet powerful change to what you're doing already whereby you can help in solving some of the world's problems with purchases you're making anyway.

Buying social is an easy way to get started with your charitable giving if you don't have much spare cash, or are not yet sure which cause to align your business with. It also enables you to support a range of social causes based on your business needs.

What is buying social?

Also known as social sourcing or impact sourcing, buying social involves consciously choosing to source the goods and services your business needs from suppliers who are charities or social enterprises. Personally, I also include employing or contracting people who have experienced some kind of challenges or deprivation in their life, for example poverty, abuse, war or neglect. That is typically those who could be at risk of needing another form of charitable aid if they are unable to turn their lives around.

The traditional corporate philanthropy model is to incur business costs and then make donations from profits, whereas buying social is a way to help social causes in the usual course of business – you don't need to make additional donations to make a difference. Though you can of course do that too! An example of an organisation that encourages social buying is Fairtrade. It was founded in 1992 to improve the treatment and prosperity of producers in the developing world. Nowadays many suppliers and buyers adopt Fairtrade standards across the globe.

Ways to incorporate social buying into your business

Using social suppliers is something you could implement immediately:

- Start by reviewing your existing suppliers and identifying which you'd be happy to replace with a social cause.

- Wait until the next time you need to buy something, and when the time comes, check out if there is a social enterprise that supplies this.

As with any commercial decision other factors are also important: such as the product or service being fit for purpose, cost and quality. And there may be times when you're unable to source a social supplier. However, there are an increasing number of social enterprises offering a business products and services.

A couple of leading social suppliers making a huge difference around the world who have really inspired me are *WildHearts and Samasource.*

WildHearts is a social enterprise that was set up in 2006 by Mick Jackson. Having almost died on a mountaineering trip he decided to embrace his second chance at life by setting himself the bold goal of transforming the lives of one million people. *WildHearts* offers business services such as stationery supplies, printing and furniture to organisations, with the income generated being put to social projects. The organisation has evolved significantly over the years and, while still supplying business services, it also provides entrepreneurial training and support, and micro-finance opportunities to people around the world. It is a growing community that has had a positive impact on the lives of over 110,000 people.

I love how *WildHearts* engage all sorts of people in their work. I was at one of their conferences recently where it was energising to be at an event with a great mix of schoolchildren, young entrepreneurs, socially-minded business owners, social enterprises and corporate leaders – all sharing common values around making the world a better place.

Samasource was set up by Leila Janah in 2008. Her vision was to match those living in poverty around the world with jobs that will pay them a better living wage, thanks to the Internet. Rather than applying the traditional charity model of giving things to people for free, their ethos is to give 'work' – to give those in poverty access to dignified jobs so they're empowered and have money to buy what they need rather than receiving hand-outs. The services offered include quality data-processing for large organisations, and a training school that equips people with digital literacy so they can set themselves up to earn money through online job portals (see social outsourcing below).

The people *Samasource* employ and train help themselves and their communities to become more sustainable, through having income they can spend, rather than being trapped in a dependency model.

I prefer to deliberately buy from those with similar values, and so explore what social suppliers are available. Sometimes I find great social suppliers; however, I also buy products and services from commercial businesses with a strong social ethos if they are a better fit for what I'm looking for.

I run a business network and I'd love to use social venues but it's not always easy to find places with the right capacity, staffing, refreshments or energy. I always first try to source social venues although if I can't find a suitable one, I'll run my events at commercial venues where the owners share similar values.

The extent to which you buy social will depend on your values and the availability of good social suppliers to meet your needs.

Just last year I decided to change my bank accounts to an ethical and caring bank and feel better for having done this.

Social outsourcing

You've probably heard of large companies outsourcing parts of their business to countries in Asia. But have you thought about how you could do this too?

I welcome how technology has given people all round the world the opportunity to increase their skills and work their way out of poverty. Some years ago I had a contract with a large American company to deliver training to all staff in their Indian office. It was a fascinating trip. On one hand it was great to see locals in relatively well paid jobs and how they talked with gratitude about the opportunities this was creating for them, and their families. But I was also so horrified by the way they I felt they were being treated and exploited by the organisation that I decided not to work for that client again. By contrast Samasource, the social enterprise I mentioned earlier, has found an ethical way to connect businesses and resources around the world.

As a small business owner, outsourcing to social enterprises or individuals who are keen to work towards a better life, can be a lovely way to make a difference. It can be also feel very rewarding, especially if you choose to get to know the people you hire, and treat them as core members of your team.

I feel a strong urge to give work to talented entrepreneurial souls, and especially others who could otherwise be one of the many we support in other ways through charitable aid. Recently I took on a wonderful woman in the Philippines to help transfer some of my courses onto a new computer system and to set up online sales funnels. Even though she was much more expensive than others who had applied I employed her because she was by far the best candidate for the job and, unlike other businesses who source from overseas to keep their costs down, I believe in paying someone for their skills at a fair global rate. It doesn't seem ethical to me to pay people less just because they live in a country with a lower cost of living. By contrast, it feels great that we're partnering as professionals and that I'm contributing to the welfare of her family – as happens when we hire others.

To clarify, you don't have to 'employ' people on a full-time permanent contract if you don't have that much work for them to do. You could instead ask that they set themselves up as self-employed so they can invoice you for their time. Or source contractors through social causes and have the cause invoice you.

Let's help more entrepreneurial souls improve their lives – by hiring them!

Where to find social suppliers

As a means of encouraging us to buy from social suppliers, Social Enterprise UK launched an initiative called *Buying Social* in 2013 that challenges individuals and businesses to consider where we buy our goods and services from.

They have a directory of social suppliers you can check out and are expanding their reach globally – with an affiliate program *Buy Social Canada* that was launched in 2015 which even gives businesses the opportunity to become certified as a *Buy Social* Purchaser.

There are several other ways to source social suppliers:

- Do a Google search – for social enterprises offering what you're looking to buy.

- Ask people in your networks.

- Contact local or national bodies for registered social enterprises or charities.

If social outsourcing is something you're interested in exploring, there are several online portals that can connect you with people who are looking for work. A couple of sites I've found good people on are:

- Up Work (https://www.upwork.com/) – I like how you can post a project or job here, invite applicants to apply, and payments are held in escrow until specific tasks or work has been delivered.

- Fiverr.com (www.fiverr.com) – this is a website where thousands of people all round the world post what they will do for US$5. Buyers are encouraged to rate and endorse suppliers, which makes it easier to select good resources. I use this site to source people to complete small tasks, e.g. transcripts, product graphics, e-book covers. Again I like to be mindful of paying a fair market rate rather than going for the cheapest resource.

There are some useful links for sourcing social buyers on my website at www.givetoprofit.com.

How to select the right social suppliers

It's good news that there are many social enterprises supplying products and services we can make use of as business owners. However, just because they are provided by a social cause, doesn't mean they are a good fit for what you're looking for, or the best solution in terms of cost, reliability, quality, etc. Obviously as with all other aspects of business, it's worth vetting people, and selecting those who are the best fit for your business. There is one social enterprise near me I'd love to support but their services are more than twice the price of similar suppliers. I'm happy to pay a premium for good services but, because there are other good options, I don't buy from them.

Likewise, while social causes are set up with the specific intention of having a social impact, the actual impact these enterprises have varies. Unlike the situation with commercial businesses, where financial results are a comparable measure of success (albeit not the only measure), it seems there are no such consistent measures in the social-impact arena.

More details on how to choose social causes to support are detailed in Chapter 9 including how to identify the impact social causes have. As a starting point, once you've identified which causes supply the resources you are looking for, check out their website to see if they give any kind of impact reporting, e.g. for every £15 you spend, a child receives free school meals for a year; the number of people they have helped; or information about how the lives of those they support typically change. The social enterprise *WildHearts* I mentioned earlier is a good example of a social enterprise that provides this kind of information.

Key Points

- Buying social is a brilliant way to make a difference in the course of business without needing to have any 'extra' money for donations – you simply make socially-conscious decisions about which suppliers you'll use to source products and services your business needs.

- You're likely to support a range of social causes by 'buying social' – because there's unlikely to be one social cause that fulfils all your business needs.

How could you have more social impact by simply changing your suppliers?

Resources

Find more resources to help you buy social on my website www.givetoprofit.com.

PART 3

The Seven Steps to Growing a Business by Supporting Charities and Social Causes

"Be the change you want to see in the world."
MAHATMA GANDHI

7

Connect to your 'WHY'

"In business it doesn't matter what you do, it matters why you do it."

SIMON SINEK, AUTHOR and THOUGHT LEADER

Everyone who supports charities and social causes has different reasons for doing so. When you connect to what's important to you and why you want to support social causes through your business, this can become a powerful beacon or guiding light that keeps you on track and helps you make choices aligned to your heart: which causes to support; what resources to allocate to charitable giving; and how to do this in a way that reflects who you are, and your business vision.

Some people think giving to others is a selfless act, and to some extent, it can be. But everybody I know who does charitable work also talks about the huge personal benefits. Common benefits include being able to connect to deeper feelings of love, gratitude, peace, satisfaction and worthiness. Charitable giving also helps put our own life challenges into perspective, can give our lives more meaning or be an opportunity to meet new people.

Here are some questions to help you get clear on your 'why':

- Why do you want to support social causes through your business?

- Why is charitable giving important to you?

- What impact would you love to have in the world or your community?

- What would you like to do?

- Do you already have a cause you'd like to support? For instance, often when people have lost a loved one to a disease, they decide they'd like to raise money to help find a cure or support others in a similar position. Maybe you feel passionately about children, the elderly, animal welfare, social justice, community development, helping those in third world countries or those who have suffered during wars or genocide, etc. There are many great causes to choose from.

- What motivates you? Is it making a difference, getting results, helping people, using your skills, making money, creating things, being around people, or any other factors? If you want to make the most of a partnership with a social cause, being passionate about the one you select will help you feel compelled to take action to support them.

- What personal needs do you have that are not currently getting met in your personal life? For instance, if you are somebody who loves spending time with young people and you don't get a lot of exposure to that on a day-to-day basis, would that be something you could do through supporting a charity or social cause? Maybe you've moved to a new area, your children have left home, you feel lonely or isolated, and you want to connect and spend time with like-minded people.

- Would you like to use your brain in a particular way? I quite often hear about people who have left the corporate world to set up their own business only to find they miss using their brains in the way they did before. Of course they are still using their brains, but just differently. A good way to get this need met is through charitable activities. I know I've really enjoyed helping social enterprises to develop strategies in areas that differ to my own business.

- How would you like to make a difference in the world?

- Do you have something else to offer that you're not currently expressing in your life such as creativity, a talent or skill?

- What do you love doing that you're not currently doing in your life, e.g. travel, spending time outdoors, cooking, art, music, singing, DIY, gardening or being around animals?

- Are you looking to get more experience in a particular field, or of something you've never done before but would love to do?

- What are you passionate about that you'd love to do more of? This may or may not be related to your work. For instance, do you have a particular hobby you did when you were younger that you're no longer doing and would love to take up again?

Of course I'm assuming your desire to support a social cause through your business is heart-driven, i.e. you're not simply doing this to get business. If you are only considering supporting a charity as a way to get more clients, stop right there! You are wasting your time – people will see through you, and your efforts will backfire. The Give-to-Profit model only works for business owners, entrepreneurs and leaders who are genuinely driven by a desire to make a difference – those who ooze kindness and love helping others.

Key Points

 You're more likely to implement ideas if they are ones that light up your heart.

 The first step to choosing the best way for you to support social causes through your business is to get clear on why you want to do this.

Social Impact Actions

Take a moment to reflect on your thoughts so far – your ideas and reasons for supporting social causes through your business – why do you want to support social causes through your business?

Note these down in the Give-to-Profit Practical Guide you can download for free at www.givetoprofit.com.

8

Define your Strategic Charitable Goal

"It's not hard to make decisions when you know what your values are."

ROY DISNEY, BUSINESSMAN

Those who set themselves highly attractive goals are more likely to succeed – as long as their thoughts, feelings, and actions are aligned to these! If you want to grow your business by supporting social causes, there are a few critical ingredients for your charitable goals. The purpose of this chapter is to explain how to set charitable goals that will benefit you, your business and your chosen cause – in ways that resonate with your business vision, and helps you demonstrate your social impact, to customers and stakeholders. By making only a couple of small changes to the way you may have set charitable goals before, you could have a much more social impact and generate more business.

As I mentioned in Chapter 2, strategically linking your charitable and business activities, is at the crux of the Give-to-Profit model. This involves setting charitable goals that will enable you to:

- Maximise your impact – it's easy enough to donate time, money or resources to good causes. However, you can have more impact when you take the time to think strategically about how to do this.

- Make smart decisions – you're more likely to make good choices about the type of charitable activities you get involved in when you do what I suggest in this chapter.

- Be more efficient – when you have a clear goal that's aligned to the impact(s) you'd like to have, you can be more focused on how you spend your time, money and resources.

- Avoid costly mistakes – all of the above will help you avoid making costly mistakes in terms of which ideas you implement or participate in.

I speak very much from personal experience here – while I've enjoyed lots of success with my charitable giving, there have also been decisions I wouldn't make again. The process I share in this book has evolved over the years. It was only once people started to ask me to help them create socially-conscious businesses that I realised I'd progressed from simply fundraising to putting social impact at the core of my business.

As I started to document the steps I'd taken, I realised when things had gone well, and exceeded my expectations, I'd followed the process I share in this book. By contrast when I'd deviated from this, I made a few mistakes.

Link your business and charitable giving strategically

So how do you link your business and charitable giving? It's easy. All you need to do is to come up with charitable activities that will benefit all three parties – you, your business and a social cause, as shown here:

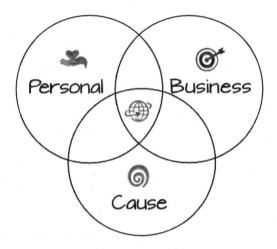

For example, if you want to raise funds for a cause through your business organise fundraisers your ideal clients or partners will enjoy and support. Rather than getting involved with random charitable events, make conscious decisions to participate in activities that will help you connect and engage with more of your ideal clients or partners.

Targeting fundraising activities specifically at your ideal clients turns fundraising into a highly effective marketing strategy. People buy from those they know, like and trust so offering an opportunity for your clients, followers and contacts to get involved in charitable projects, will help you connect and build stronger relationships with them – particularly those who share similar values and ideals. This will influence what people remember and think about you – your personal brand – and help you be more memorable to those you meet.

Targeting fundraising activities specifically at your ideal clients turns fundraising into a highly effective marketing strategy.

Let me give you an example of how offering fundraisers to my audience has influenced decisions I've made. When I first started out raising funds for my trips to Rwanda, I had lots of people offering to help me out with my fundraising, for example by suggesting charity balls or other social events where we could all invite our friends along. It was very kind of these people to offer their support but I didn't want to organise those types of event as my family and friends were already supporting me in many different ways and they all had very different interests. There was no obvious way to appeal to them all. I was also spending too much time working and not spending enough time just having fun with my family and close friends. So the thought of taking on the planning of social fundraising events, which would eat into my personal space, didn't appeal.

I was very clear I wanted my fundraising activities to be linked to my business. Not because I had any expectation or hope that my business would benefit, that didn't even cross my mind. It just felt an easier way to slot my fundraising into my already busy life.

Your social impact vision

Whether you want to raise funds for a particular cause or project, to volunteer or put social giving at the heart of our business, it's worth considering your 'big picture' vision before defining your charitable goals.

What social impact would you love to have through your business?

My initial goal was to raise enough funds for Project LIGHT Rwanda through my business to sponsor a young person for a year and cover the cost of my trips. Now I'd love to have a positive impact on the lives of one million people – this statement has effectively become a social impact mission statement for my business. Some of this will be satisfied through the type of work I do and selling books. But I also set myself charitable goals aligned to this each year.

- What social impact would you love to have?

- What type of charitable giving appeals to you most?

- To what extent do you want to integrate charitable giving into your business?

- How could you summarise this in one sentence or statement?

Your strategic charitable goal

Once you have a social-impact vision, it's time to define a shorter-term goal, typically for six to twelve months, aligned to this, one you can easily work towards, measure and communicate to your customers and stakeholders.

To do this I'm going to explain how to define your charitable goals and other desired outcomes from three different perspectives – for you, your business and the cause you want to support.

Define your charitable goal

As you'll now be aware, there are many different types of charitable goals you could set yourself including:

- To raise a specific amount of money for a cause

- To help a certain number of people

- To provide a certain number of items to a cause, e.g. books, school uniforms, meals, etc.

- To organise a fundraising event in aid of a social cause

- To take on a non-exec role

- To source 50% of your supplies from social enterprises or businesses with similar values

- To volunteer for a local cause

- To volunteer for a charity overseas

- To organize a social project, e.g. to build a school or set up a library.

Before committing to anything it's worth considering what you want to contribute (e.g. time, money, resources), what you enjoy doing, and how you intend to be while doing this.

For instance, if you're wanting to add meaning to your life, you're likely to enjoy a far greater emotional bond and greater satisfaction when you get actively involved with a cause rather than simply making financial donations. Questions to ask yourself include:

- How much time would I like to spend supporting causes through my business?

- What skills or knowledge would I like to share?

- How do I intend to be – a passive or proactive supporter?

- How much money would I like to invest in achieving this goal?

- What doubts or fears would I like to overcome?

- How else would I like to contribute to a cause?

- If you have more time than money at the moment, you may want to consider donating your time. Conversely, if you're short on time but have plenty money, you may want to only make financial donations. Or you could do what I've done which was to remodel my business to free up more time and money to be out 'in the field' doing humanitarian trips and fundraising.

When deciding how much time you want to spend on this, remember to be kind to yourself too by making sure you only take on what you have the capacity to do. Be mindful too that if you adapt what you're already doing in the course of business, for example by replacing some marketing activities with fundraising events, or socially sourcing suppliers, you may be able to have social impact without spending any extra time or money.

When setting your goals, I suggest using the 'SMARTA' format so you have more of a focus and something you can share with those interested in your social impact:

- **Specific** – your goal is detailed enough to know what you're working towards, e.g. 'to raise £20,000' is more specific than 'to raise funds for charity'.

- **Measureable** – there is a clear way you can measure your progress/results and demonstrate this to your customers and stakeholders (see Chapter 12).

- **Achievable** – you have the resources to make this happen (time, money, and whatever else you need).

- **Relevant** – aligned to your big picture vision and what's important to you (both personally and for your business).

- **Time-bound** – be specific in the way you define this, e.g. '31st December 2016' rather than the vagueness of 'this year'. When setting a long-term goal remember also to break it down into to smaller chunks (action steps), and define these in a similar format.

- **Actionable** – a goal you can take action towards. Here are some examples of charitable goals in this format:

  - To raise US$25,000 for Create Global Healing by 31st December 2012.

  - To go on an overseas humanitarian trip by 31st December 2010.

  - To become a charity trustee by 31st May 2016.

  - To supply school uniforms for 1,000 children in Africa by 30th December 2017.

You may find it easier to define your charitable goals using the goal setting template in the Give-to-Profit Practical Guide that accompanies this book, available at www.givetoprofit.com.

Define your desired outcomes: for you personally

Once you've defined your charitable goal, the next step is to identify your desired outcomes so you can consider these when evaluating which charitable idea(s) best complement your business.

Your answers are likely to be very similar to your reasons for supporting a charity as we covered in the last chapter. That said, I suggest defining your personal desired outcomes each time you set yourself a strategic charitable goal, as these change over time. Ask yourself:

- How specifically would I like to benefit from achieving this goal?

- How would I like to feel?

- How would I like to grow personally?

- What would I like to experience?

- What would make this worthwhile?

- What would make this goal more exciting or compelling?

- What would energise me?

- What do I love doing?

- Who do I love spending time with?

Define your desired outcomes: for your business

Now it's time to look at things from the perspective of how you'd like your business to benefit.

- What positive impact would you like your charitable giving to have on your business?

- What goals are you already working towards?

- What activities do you currently have planned that you could add a charitable component to?

- How would you like to *grow* your business?

- What new products or services could you trial?

- What would make the biggest difference to your business?

- How do you measure the *success* or growth of your business? This could include value of sales, volume of sales, number of clients, or an increase in revenue or profits.

- How do you measure the *visibility* of your business? For example, number of leads in the pipeline, number of email subscribers, email engagement, blog readers, number of group members, social media contacts, social media engagement, public speaking opportunities, interview opportunities, YouTube video viewing figures, etc.

- What needs to change in your business?

When fundraising I often test demand for potential new products or services by offering tasters or pilots for donations. I did this a few years ago when I needed to raise money for one of my trips to Rwanda. I'd meditated on the quickest and easiest way to raise the cash and the idea that came to mind was to run a two-day workshop, teaching people how to take their workshops online. This was something I knew I could easily pull together, and so I decided to suss out interest in a Facebook group I run. I simply put up a post inviting members to spend two days with me learning how to create online courses, in return for a donation of at least £100. I was stunned that within only a couple of hours I had a full workshop and waiting list. But I was even more surprised about what happened afterwards. During the workshop, I became aware that most attendees wanted ongoing help to ensure they implemented what they'd learnt. So at the end of the workshop I asked if they'd like me to run a mastermind group that would meet up for a couple of hours a month – eight of the ten signed up on the spot!

What had started out as an event to fund a humanitarian trip to Rwanda delivered far more than that. As well as raising the funds I needed I also generated an immediate increase in monthly revenue and had discovered there was demand for a new course. I have since run the workshop again and have also recently launched an online version. So in this example, my primary goal was to raise funds for my trip while also exploring the potential of a new product idea.

I'll be sharing ideas for how you can achieve your strategic charitable goals in the next chapter so don't worry about deciding how you'll do this yet. At this stage simply consider how you'd like your business to benefit as a consequence of your charitable activities.

Define your desired outcomes: for the cause

How would you like the cause to benefit from your support? There may be several ways you'd like the cause to benefit. Examples include:

- Funds donated or raised

- Increased visibility (e.g. more media coverage or a greater presence on social media platforms)

- New funding opportunities or grants

- New supporters who pledge regular donations

- New supporters on their database

- Resources the cause could use to generate future income

- New volunteers, board members, ambassadors or strategic partners

- Opportunities to tell their story.

The easiest way to come up with a goal and desired outcomes for the charity is to ask them what they'd like help with, and to discuss your ideas with them.

It's also worth considering the actual impact you'd like to make in terms of how your support changes the lives of people or makes a difference to the planet.

Identify your critical success factors

Once you have a charitable goal and list of desired outcomes it's time to identify the most important outcomes that reflect a mix of personal, charitable and business benefits – what I call your critical success factors.

Why? Because having this clarity will help you come up with ideas that are aligned with what's most important to you, and guide you towards making objective business decisions when it comes to deciding how to achieve your goal. Defining your critical success factors at this stage also makes it easier to measure the impact of your charitable giving, as I discuss in Chapter 12.

Key Points

- The right charitable goal for you depends on your 'why', resources you've got access to, and the extent to which you'd like to integrate social giving into your business.

- If you want to grow your business by supporting charities or social causes the critical component to get in place is to link your business and your charitable activities strategically.

  Where you want to raise funds for a cause, this means coming up with fundraising events that appeal to large numbers of your ideal clients or business partners.

❤️ Defining your charitable goal and desired outcomes from the three perspectives of yourself, your business and cause, means you'll have factors to consider when deciding how to achieve your goal. You can also then use these to measure and demonstrate your impact to your customers and other stakeholders.

 Social Impact Actions

Before considering how to achieve your charitable goal, take a few moments to define your goal, desired outcomes and critical success factors. There's a template for doing this in the Give-to-Profit Practical Guide that accompanies this book. You can download this for free at www.givetoprofit.com.

NEXT STEPS:

If you've not yet decided which cause to support, carry on reading the next chapter for tips on how to choose one aligned to your heart.

If you already know what cause you're going to support, go to Chapter 10 to start coming up with ideas for how to achieve your goal.

9

How to Choose a Charity or Social Cause to Support

"It ain't what you give, it's the way that you give it."

CAROLINE FIENNES, CHARITABLE-GIVING EXPERT and AUTHOR

Many people ask me how to choose a charity or social cause to support through their business. Some common questions are:

- Should the cause be one in a similar field as your business?

- Is it better to pick one you one feel passionately about?

- Or one that's most likely to appeal to your audience?

- Is it OK to support more than one cause?

There is no right and wrong, however if you want to donate money, raise funds or volunteer your time, I suggest you pick just one primary cause to support in this way initially. Why? Because it means you can build a closer relationship with them, make better use of your time and money, and it's easier for those you meet to understand what's important to you. This in turn will help you build stronger connections with those who resonate with similar causes.

Yes, you may support several causes in different ways, for example you may have one cause you raise funds for and others who are 'social' suppliers and that's fine: the causes you buy from in most cases are likely to be different from those you raise funds for or volunteer with (see Chapter 6 for information on how to source social suppliers). But when you're just starting out with charitable giving through your business and want to donate money, raise funds or volunteer I'd suggest focussing on supporting one main cause initially. The focus of this chapter is to help you do this.

If you've already chosen your preferred cause you may want to go straight to the next chapter. Though you are welcome keep reading to reaffirm your choice, or to find out criteria that can also help you make smart choices when social sourcing.

One of the things I'll be discussing is how to give well – supporting causes that are effective in serving those they are aiming to help. There are plenty poorly run causes and I therefore suggest you do your due diligence so you can make informed decisions about the causes you support. Sometimes, in the course of life, opportunities will present themselves that touch your heart and compel you to act, without any need to look into them further. For example, I recently decided to run an online fundraising event to raise funds for a friend's son to build a house for a homeless family in Malawi. She's been a great friend for years and I simply wanted to support the good efforts of her son. Making the decision to do this on a one-off basis was simply something I wanted to do, because I knew I could help. Likewise, quite a few people in my business network have organised fundraisers and other relief projects in response to the Syrian Refugee

Crisis in Europe, even though they already have strong connections to other causes.

As with many other aspects of your business, you can decide when to go with your heart versus doing more thorough checks.

Some people ask whether they should involve staff, followers or clients to help select a cause to support. While this can be a good thing for larger businesses, if you run a small business it is really important the main cause you support is one that touches your heart. With a small business, your personal and business 'brands' are inter-linked. The causes you support and how you do this become part of your story – what people think, say, remember about you and ask you about. As a solo-preneur your choice of cause is a reflection of you. When you're enthusiastic about the cause you're supporting through your business, you're more likely to remain committed to it – so I suggest either making the decision yourself or at least coming up with a shortlist you'd love to support if you really do want to involve others in the decision.

Use this process to select a primary cause to support:

1. Define your desired outcomes
2. Decide how you want to contribute
3. Do your research
4. Decide on the charity to support

Step 1: Get clear on your desired outcomes

This partly relates to why you want to support social causes through your business and charitable goals you've set yourself (as we covered in Chapters 7 and 8). However, there are also more specific factors to consider in relation to the type of cause you'd like to support.

What type of cause would you love to support?

You may have ideas for this already but if not, here are a few things to consider:

- **Focus** – the purpose of the cause and scope of its activities.

- **Size** – the size of the organisation can be measured in many ways including the number of people employed, number of people or creatures it helps, its geographic reach, the value of its charitable funds, etc.

- **Locality** – where the cause is based, and operates.

- **Resources** – how the cause spends, invests and distributes its resources (including money).

- **Legal entity** – whether a registered charity, foundation or non-profit; a social enterprise or an unrecognised cause close to your heart.

Let's look at each of these in more detail:

FOCUS: What is the best focus of cause for you to support?

The most common question people ask me is whether they should support a cause with a similar scope and focus as their business, or to pick one that focuses on something completely different. The answer really does depend on 'why' you want to support a cause and the extent to which you'd like to be involved.

Supporting a cause with the same focus as your business can be a great way to offer your services to people who can't afford to pay for them. And this can help to raise your visibility as an expert in your field.

I know opticians in the UK who volunteer their services through charities in areas of the world where people struggle to get access to good eye care or can't afford it.

I also have a friend who runs a laughter club purely to raise funds for a cause close to her heart. She's clear the club is her gift to the world. Raising funds in this way has been important to her and as a by-product of this, she is perceived as a compassionate laughter expert, which has helped her attract paying clients.

However some people find it hard to apply clear boundaries for distinguishing between what they charge for as against what they offer on a charitable basis, when they pick a cause which has a focus similar to that of their business.

I've had people tell me they've met people who support charities just to get business but I wouldn't worry about this. As I've said before, people see through anyone doing this, so as long as you're coming from a place of love, kindness and compassion, and demonstrating this through your actions, you'll be fine.

Another potential downside of supporting a cause with the same focus as your business could be that you may be missing out on an opportunity to get other personal needs met. When you support a cause with very different activities to your business, you may discover new skills or talents and skills you didn't know you had. Volunteering in an area very different to your business could also help stimulate fresh ideas for how your business could evolve into something more aligned to your heart. Supporting a charity that's different from your business can also help you switch off from the 'norm' of your day-to-day life.

The downside of supporting a cause which has a very different focus to your business is that there may be less potential to joint-venture with them. That said, you just don't know what supporters they have or how they may be looking to expand or grow. So I wouldn't be put off choosing a cause that has a completely different focus to your business.

Irrespective of the scope of the cause, what's more important is that your choice engages your heart! That you select a cause you're excited about becoming involved with and that's aligned with the legacy you'd like to leave in this world. When you support a cause that's close to your heart, this deep heartfelt connection will help you continue to feel motivated and authentically put charitable giving at core of your business over the long-term.

If you select a cause that's a good fit with your values, needs, motivations and goals, you'll expand your network of like-minded people, this will make you feel good, and you'll be making a difference, irrespective of whether the scope of the cause are related to your business.

Here are some questions you may find helpful:

- Do you want to support a cause that conducts research?

- Or would you prefer to support a cause that is more action-focused?

- Do you want to support a cause that supports charitable activities from a distance?

- Or do you want the cause to be more active 'in the field'?

SIZE: What size of cause would you like to work with?

Would you prefer to work with and support a small or large cause? There are obviously pros and cons of each. When you connect and work with a small cause, you may be able to get more highly involved in what they're doing. It can often be easier to understand the scope of their work, what's actually going on, their priorities, and to build strong relationships with the key players. By contrast, when you work with and support a larger organisation, they may have broader reach or have more resources available to them.

LOCALITY: Where does the cause operate?

Your preference is likely to relate to your reasons for supporting a charitable cause in the first place.

- Do you want to support a charity that is local to you, so you feel you can get involved, and feel part of a force for good within your local community?

- Or would you prefer to be part of a global movement by supporting an international cause?

And of course there are also large international charities or not-for-profit organisations with local branches.

RESOURCES: How does the cause allocate resources?

Many people have the belief that they prefer to support charities where most of the money goes directly to those in need. I used to think this too, until I realised its many flaws.

Expecting causes to have low operating costs infers the expectation that people doing good in the world, should work for free, or not be paid well: that money should not be spent on administrative or operational costs. But how can any professional organisation be effective under those restraints? Especially if you're trying to operate internationally, in third world countries or those devastated by war or natural disaster, where distribution costs are often very high due to a lack of infrastructure?

It feels like a dose of cultural madness! Especially when many of those with this mindset expect to be paid for doing their own jobs or to receive state benefits, whether or not they contribute to society? I'm sure most of those with this view wouldn't be happy if they were expected to work for nothing, or to contribute to society in return for benefits (other than those in genuine critical need of them obviously). There has been a backlash in recent years of performance-based pay yet I wonder how different the world would be if it was culturally acceptable to reward people based on their contribution to society.

If a cause is to have the greatest possible impact this requires resources, investment in skilled people, technology, training, security, systems, offices, distribution and other operating costs typical of any organisation. Yes many of those working for causes are unpaid volunteers who do great work but there is often the need for well-paid specialists too.

Having a low cost-base isn't a measure of efficiency or impact. If the purpose of the cause is to send tents to those who need them, they will need reliable distribution channels in order to ensure the tents arrive at the desired destination, and in a timely manner. To not invest in these good distribution services could result in the tents never arriving, or turning up too late.

To choose a social cause based solely on operational or admin costs is like selecting a drug based on the one with the lowest production cost rather than the one that will heal a particular symptom or illness.

Efficiency, effectiveness and social impact are far more meaningful criteria to consider when choosing a charity to support, rather than simply their operational costs.

LEGAL ENTITY: What type do you want to support?

You may not yet have any preference about the type of cause you want to support but it is worth noting at this stage that registered charities and not-for-profit organisations are, in most countries, governed by tighter legislation than social enterprises, community projects or unregistered social causes. This means there could be implications for you, your business and the charity, depending on what you want to do – particularly if you want to raise funds for a charity (as I explain in Chapter 5). From a practical perspective there are different registers for each type of cause.

Of course there is no requirement to support only registered charities or formal social enterprises. For example, you may wish to support a more informal charitable cause such as someone doing good in your community; someone who has adopted children (which to me is one of the most charitable 'deeds' anyone can do); someone who is struggling to raise the costs of medical care; local community groups or schools; or someone who has lost a loved one which is impacting on their income. There are likely to be many people around you who could do with help.

Let me share how I got clear on the type of cause I wanted to connect with.

Because I'm motivated to make a difference I knew I wanted to 'give back' in some way but I also believed I needed to generate a good income first and so focussed initially on building a sustainable business. It wasn't a surprise to find that once my business was doing well, I then felt there was something missing.

When I asked myself the extent to which I wanted to be involved with a cause, I knew it was to be more than simply making financial donations. I already supported quite a few charities in this way by making regular donations but didn't feel emotionally attached to them.

Over the years, whenever I saw footage on the TV of natural disasters or those affected by war, I felt useless because I don't have skills that could really make a difference in those critical moments. Yes I make financial donations, but there was another need within me that wasn't getting met.

Personally, I'd also wanted to have children, but for various reasons, this didn't happen. That left a gaping hole in my life as I felt I had so much more love in my heart to share with others. I also knew there had to be other ways that I could help young people.

When I took the time to consider my 'why' and desired outcomes, it became clear that I wanted to be involved with a cause that supported young people, that used some of my skills, and would give me the opportunity to travel (my number one passion).

Other factors important to me were to have opportunities to get out there in the field, working directly with the young people, to be connecting with them in a face-to-face setting, and to feel I was really making a difference.

I also wanted to work with a small cause so I could really get to know all those involved and help shape what they were doing. And I wanted to work with people who shared my values and dreams for a better world.

Step 2: Decide how you want to contribute

Once you're clear on the reasons you'd like to 'give' through your business, and the type of cause you'd like to support, the next step is to consider how you'd like to contribute to a cause. Do you want to volunteer your time, support them financially or with other resources?

You may already be clear on this but if not, reflect on your reasons for wanting to support a social cause, as we covered in the last couple of chapters.

Doing this will help you identify causes that will be a good fit for you.

Step 3: Do your research

A critical step in deciding which cause to support is to do your research. You want to be able to make informed decisions that will enable you to support social causes that are well managed, make the most of your support and satisfy your reasons for doing this in the first place. The level of research you do is personal. What's important is that you at least check out what's important to you.

Some people don't do the same level of research for causes connected to them personally as they would for an unknown cause but remember whatever decision you make in terms of who you choose to support is a reflection of your business. I'm someone who naturally trusts people until they give me cause for concern. However, it's still prudent to check out at least the basic facts – just as you would check out business partners or suppliers. I'm sure you don't want to be associated with a social cause that ends up in the press for the wrong reasons! So make sure you research how the organisation is registered, structured, governed, the impact they are actually having and whether you share similar values.

What to research

Some people like to gather facts and figures by doing what's called secondary research – reviewing accounts, journals, reports and information available on the Internet. Others prefer to gather their own (primary) research by getting out there and speaking to people.

The types of things to research include:

- What is the purpose or mission of the cause?

- What governance structures are in place?

- Who are the management team?

- What experience do they have?

- What is the scope of the cause's activities?

- How is the cause funded?

- What press coverage has there been?

- What are people saying about the cause on social media?

- How is the cause performing financially?

- What tangible results is the cause getting?

- What challenges are they facing?

- What are their plans for the next few years?

- How do they fit with your reasons for supporting a social cause?

- Do you seem a good fit personally with what they're looking for?

- If they are potential social suppliers, what do their existing customers say about them?

- How do they measure and report their impact and the results they are getting from their efforts?

- What awards have they won?

It's also worth researching the actual difference the cause is making in relation to its mission, goals and the field it's operating in.

There are many charities and social causes set up with good intentions but which unfortunately do not deliver the impact they'd hoped. In the worst cases, good intentions can actually make things worse for those on the ground. One of the main models for charitable giving in the 1970s was to give hand-outs to those in need rather than provide longer-term solutions. However, it's now widely recognised that giving hand-outs over the long-term breeds co-dependency rather than sustainability.

The impact a cause is having is influenced by many things including the scope of its activities, for example whether it nurtures a few future leaders through education, or invests the same funds in providing mosquito nets to hundreds of families.

There is no right or wrong when it comes to whether you help lots of people directly, or choose to support fewer future leaders or key players who will touch the lives of many others. However, it is important to check out the impact that causes you're considering are having and whether they are getting good results or wasting resources.

Because I like to see results I can remember feeling frustrated that a local social enterprise (with a high profile leader) seemed to get a lot of money to carry out research to address several social issues. They certainly produced some interesting reports but over the years I don't remember seeing any actual positive impact or tangible benefits from their work. Not surprisingly the enterprise no longer exists.

Where to find causes to support

There are many different ways to find charitable partners:

- Your existing networks

  Ask your network of friends, family and business contacts if they know any causes that fit your criteria. Remember, your networks are both those you know personally and through your business.

- Governing organisations

  In most countries you can find out key information about formal charitable entities through public records or professional bodies, e.g. registered charities, not-for-profits, social enterprises and B-corps (or any other name for these).

- Portal websites

  There are quite a few websites that list various social causes I've listed some of these on my website at www.givetoprofit. com.

- Social media groups

  Put out a request in a group you are a member of on social media, e.g. "I'm looking to find a cause that focuses on this particular type of work. Does anybody know of any that do this?"

- The Internet

  Google the type of cause you'd like to support; search groups and causes on Facebook, LinkedIn, YouTube or on 'Meet Up'.

  A couple of years ago I wanted to do something for the homeless. So I started to explore what opportunities there were for me to get involved with. Not specifically through my business, but more at a personal level. I searched through Facebook and discovered The Rucksack Project. A charitable project where individuals fill a rucksack with lots of goodies, e.g. clothes, a sleeping bag and flask, that is then given out to a homeless person.

- Your local community

  Check with your library, on notice boards or community magazines for local clubs, projects or causes.

- Volunteering

  If like me, you find facts and figures helpful but also like to get a feel for people or a project, then volunteering is a great way to do this. I know I make better decisions when I meet people and experience their work. Having an emotional connection with those involved is as important as the cause's reputation and sustainability.

- Reach out and speak to people

  Having conversations with a range of people associated with the cause (e.g. supporters, staff, beneficiaries, etc.) can give you a really good feel for what a cause is about, the impact they have and current needs.

- Setting your intention

If you're someone who embraces the power of the Universe or the Law of Attraction, you'll understand how miracles often happen when you get clarity about what you'd like to attract into your life – that opportunities will present themselves to you, when you set your intention (state exactly what you'd like) and align your energy vibration to this. I write more about this in my book *Heartatude: The 9 Principles of Heart-Centered Success.*

That's exactly what happened for me:

Literally the day after I defined my desired outcomes for the type of humanitarian work I wanted to do, and set an intention for the perfect opportunity to present itself to me, an email about Project LIGHT Rwanda, appeared in my in-box.

The way I live my life is to follow up on such 'signs' or opportunities. So I reached out to Dr Lori Leyden who runs the charity saying: "I love the video, and I would love to hear more about the work you're doing."

She came back to me straight away and suggested we speak. During our call I immediately connected with Lori and her vision. I asked about the scope of the project, the type of people involved and the type of help they needed.

Only a few weeks later I went to Rwanda, because I knew that if I wanted to invest my time and money in supporting a charity over the long-term, I wanted to get first-hand experience of the work they were doing and to know I would connect with the rest of the team. That first trip got me hooked – to Rwanda, to the people the charity supports, and with all those involved in the project.

Once you've come up with a few potential causes to support the next step is obviously to decide which to go with.

Step 4: Decide which cause to support

Phew! Now it's time to decide which cause to support.

Of course if, like me, you only have one strong contender, this is likely to be an easy decision to make, as long as your research concludes supporting it would be a smart move. However, if you're considering more than one charity, a really good way to determine which is the best fit for you is to review them all relative to your 'critical success factors' identified in the last chapter.

I use a great decision-making matrix to help me make more complex decisions like this (and many decisions in my personal life too). The Give-to-Profit Practical Guide that accompanies this book contains a template for doing this (available for free at www.givetoprofit.com).

Once you've decided which charity to support it's time to consider how you'd like to do this, as we'll explore in the next chapter.

Frequently asked questions

Can I support more than one cause at a time?

As I mentioned earlier, if you are a small business I suggest you focus on supporting one cause initially, especially if you want to get involved in its work or do fundraising for them. If you want to make donations to a few different causes, to source social suppliers or donate to others' fundraising activities in ways that don't take up any more of your time, that's quite easy to do. But where you're building up a relationship with a cause or fundraising on its behalf I'd suggest working with one at a time.

If you decide to 'buy social' you're unlikely to find one social cause that fulfils all your business needs and so by selecting the right suppliers you'll probably end up supporting a few causes. I support different social causes in various ways through my business. When I rent rooms for talks, workshops and networking events I prefer to use facilities provided by causes. I sometimes employ local young people without jobs to help with social media and the techie side of my business. I have a couple of causes I regularly raise funds for too.

How long 'should' I support a cause for?

That really is up to you though again if you want to commit to support one main cause I'd suggest committing to it for at least a year – unless they are looking for a shorter commitment. No decision you make is permanent. You may decide to raise funds or make donations to one main cause, and then support also other social causes on an ad-hoc basis. For example the main charity I've supported for the last few years (doing fundraising and volunteering) is called Create Global Healing. However, I've also supported many other charitable causes when asked to support my friends, clients, business partners and local projects. And I consciously choose to source social suppliers where possible.

Can I really grow my business by supporting social causes?

Of course, there are already many profitable social enterprises – both those set up formally as a social cause and also commercial businesses who chose to embed social impact into their business activities. Your business can easily benefit from charitable activities if you have a sound business, which offers marketable products or services people want to buy. However, charitable giving isn't going to fix a weak product or poorly managed business.

Key Points

 You're more likely to build a good relationship with a cause and enjoy the benefits of supporting them if you choose one close to your heart – whether this is in the same or different field to your business.

 Before deciding which cause to support, get clear on the type of cause you'd like to support, and extent to which you'd like to do this. Doing this will help you identify a cause that's a good fit for you and your business.

 While you may support a number of causes in different ways (such as donating money or social sourcing), if you're going to volunteer or raise funds for a charity, there can be great benefits in only raising funds for one charity at a time.

Social Impact Actions

Note your desired outcomes for supporting a cause, the qualities of your ideal cause and the extent to which you'd like to offer support. Then do your research and choose a cause that's a good match. Remember there are practical exercises to help you do this in the Give-to-Profit Practical Guide that accompanies this book. You can download this for free at www.givetoprofit.com.

Other Resources

I've listed a few useful portal websites to use when searching for causes to support at www.givetoprofit.com.

Come up With Compelling Ideas

"Ideas spend eternity swirling around us, searching for available and willing human partners."

ELIZABETH GILBERT

Now it's time to get your creative juices flowing! To unleash your imagination and come up with ideas for how you could achieve your charitable goal.

Most of my followers want to raise funds for charitable causes and so, with that in mind, the examples I share in this chapter mainly relate to fundraising. However, the process I share to come up with ideas is one that can be used for all areas of your business, not just those relating to giving.

With so many possibilities it's always worth brainstorming a few different ideas before selecting those that are the best for you and your business. So you don't put any unnecessary pressure on yourself.

Without doubt the simplest and most successful idea I've had for fundraising is making and selling Miracle Bead Bracelets. What started as a small idea in 2010, not only still brings pleasure to many around the world, it's also raised thousands for charity.

When I started out I didn't realise they'd be so popular. I just wanted to come up with something I'd enjoy making, that people would want to impulse-buy and that would tap into the creative part of me I hadn't used for years. I'd seen someone else making bracelets for charity and thought, 'I could do that'. I came up a few designs to test the market, and then took my creations along to networking events in the hope people would buy them. It was such a pleasant surprise that people loved them! They not only bought bracelets then and there, they offered to host fundraising parties with their friends and clients, and invited me to speak at networking events and conferences.

But even better than that, as people wore the bracelets, others asked where to get them and so the ripple started to spread – people I'd never met started getting in touch and buying them too. From a business perspective I'd inadvertently become more memorable and was attracting clients and business partners who resonated with what I was doing. The fact that many of the people who have the bracelets wear them every day, also means I'm constantly in their mind, so they remember me and are more likely to get in touch if they ever need my services.

My top five fundraising ideas

I share fifty-two ways to raise funds for charity through your business in Chapter 4, with the following being my top five (in terms of raising the most funds for the least amount effort while also being enjoyable and contributing to the growth of my business):

• Selling my miracle bracelets

As I've mentioned, coming up with a low cost tangible product people will impulse-buy (as a gift or treat for themselves) is great for raising funds for charity and making you more memorable. Selling these at events where you are also showcasing your products, services or experience can do wonders for boosting your revenue too – people have another reason to come and speak to you.

• Running fundraising events that showcase your knowledge, products or services

Showcase your offerings to groups of your ideal clients while at the same time enjoying a good time with like-minded souls. Events could be in-person or online, and work really well if you want to give people the opportunity to sample what you offer – this year I've run a few online training events in this way. Sometimes I invite other business suppliers who serve the same audience to showcase their skills or products too perhaps with a talk, stand or demos. They usually promote the event to their audience, which means we all get more exposure, and raise more funds for charity too.

When I run in-person events, I take along my bracelets, invite people to sign up to one of my free resources (e.g. e-books, tip-sheets). Sometimes I also hold a raffle to raise more funds.

- Running a pilot/testing products

A few years ago I wanted to raise funds for a trip to Rwanda at fairly short notice so I put up a post in one of my Facebook groups asking if anyone would be interested in spending two days with me, learning how to create online courses, in return for donations. I hadn't planned anything in advance, i.e. I had no course outline or webpage for this: I just asked the question. And in two hours I'd filled the course, and had a waiting list of people for another one – which I charged market rates for.

Not only did I raise the funds I needed for the trip, and got great testimonials, most of the attendees subsequently signed up to a paid monthly mentoring group to help them implement what they'd learnt. Again I hadn't planned to offer ongoing support, but through responding to what attendees said they wanted, I was able to generate a new monthly revenue stream. I'd also created a marketable new workshop I've run again, and have since turned into an online course too.

- Host a film screening

We had a wonderful evening in Edinburgh a few years ago when I hosted the Scottish Film Premiere of a film called *Choice Point*. We booked a private cinema (with red carpet), held a drinks reception with a raffle, had a Q&A session with the author of the book that accompanied the film, and of course sold more bracelets! Again this helped me grow my network and introduced me to new people who have since become clients. I share more about how we scoped out this idea in the next chapter.

- Holding an online auction

The second fundraiser I did was an online auction. I asked contacts in my business network if they'd like to donate a product or experience to an auction and was amazed by the generosity of many people who decided to get involved. It was good fun, raised almost US$3,000 and again helped me build relationships with people in my community and connect with people I hadn't known previously.

Factors for consideration

Before coming up with ideas for how you could achieve your charitable goal, consider the following:

- Potential resources

- Current planned business activities

- New potential business opportunities.

Review potential resources

You are likely to have access to far more resources than you think. While at the same time you're also likely to have restraints (e.g. time and money). So it's worth noting all the potential resources available to you – your own personal resources plus those available through your business, and the cause.

Personal resources

The resources you're happy to commit to achieving your goal:

- Time

- Money

- Skills and knowledge

- Family, friends and other contacts in your personal networks (e.g. clubs, school, workplaces, etc.)

- Assets – property, valuables, computers, etc.

- Clutter – things you no longer use that could be sold for cash or donated to others.

  I remember one of the first things I did when I started fundraising was to go through cupboards, the attic and my jewellery box identifying items I then sold on eBay and at pawnbrokers. Not only was it great to turn what I wasn't using into cash, it also felt good to have cleared clutter from around the house.

I like to review my personal resources each time I set a charitable goal. This way I don't over extend myself.

Business resources

Likewise you're likely to have resources in and through your business you could make use of:

- Time – any capacity you or your team have

- Money – what would you be willing to invest to achieve this?

- Skills and knowledge – of all those involved in your business

- Products and services – your existing offerings

- Old stock or products – don't waste these if you can sell them (even at a huge discount) to generate cash

- Assets – property, valuables, technology, software, etc.

- Your email list or database – one of the greatest business assets you can build

- Your clients – what would they be interested in? And how could they help or support your efforts?

- Your followers and leads – those with whom you have good relationships

- Business partners – including the resources they may be happy to make available to you

- Your business network – including those you're connected to on social media

- Other communities where you've got a good presence or reputation

- Social causes in your network that could support your business or idea.

Charitable resources

When looking to collaborate closely with social suppliers or those you donate resources to, you could find out what resources they have you could tap into. For example, the cause's community, followers, email list, premises, assets, contacts, specialist areas of expertise, etc. It's often easier to do this once you have built a good relationship with a cause but it is worth exploring when you connect too.

Please be aware there could be tax or legal implications for a cause if they support certain activities, especially if you're fundraising for them (see Chapter 5).

Consider current planned business activities

If you want to get the best return on your time and money, the easiest way to support social causes is to adapt something you're already doing, or planning to do.

As I've already mentioned, buying social is one of the best examples of this as it's simply about sourcing what you need in the course of business from social suppliers (see Chapters 3 and 6).

Another easy thing to do is to introduce a fundraising element to:

- 'Business as usual' activities

- Events

- Product, service or book launches

- Talks and interviews

- Collaborative ventures with business partners.

One of the things I love doing is public speaking. As well as getting paid to speak at large events, I used to offer free talks in my local community, in the hope these would lead to more paid opportunities. But they rarely did. Why? Because the act of offering to speak for free meant that I was attracting groups who didn't want to pay for speakers, and often spoke to audiences who didn't want to put their hands in their pockets. Very occasionally I'd get good business leads but, in the main, I didn't find speaking for free was good use of my time – partly because I don't believe in selling 'from the stage' and at that time didn't have any low cost products, such as a book, those in the audiences I was speaking to would impulse buy.

When you ask groups for charitable donations, the whole energy around the event changes. The simple act of offering to speak on a charitable basis creates an energy exchange that results in better dynamics:

- People who may not have signed up to a free event, do sign up to fundraising events because they want to support you and the cause.

- I've found attendance rates are higher for fundraiser events than free events (typically a high percentage of those who register for free events don't show up).

- Sometimes both organisers and the attendees make donations which spreads the costs and can mean you raise more funds.

- Attendees of fundraisers are far more likely to buy something else at the event than those who go along to free events – whether you offer a fundraising product, or one of your standard products/services.

- Nowadays I very rarely do free speaking gigs but instead get paid to speak where the organisers are charging an attendance fee or if the event is for an organisation that pays its staff salaries. Or for voluntary groups I ask for donations (and travel expenses).

Consider new potential business

I love using fundraising as a way to explore the potential of new products, services or activities I could offer in the future. I find offering regular fundraisers is one of my preferred marketing strategies as they are a great way to engage and build relationships with those in my community, and brings a human touch to marketing – especially in the online business world, where personal heart connections are often neglected.

Recently I've really enjoyed organising online training events as fundraisers. My intention for these events is to raise as much money for a cause as possible and so I deliver content based on what my audience say they want – without any attachment to what could happen after the events. Although where I've had a few different topics to choose from I sometimes pick those I could monetise in the future. Some of these events are only offered on a one-off basis while others have evolved into new products too.

Alternatively you could create a new 'fundraising' product, i.e. one where all proceeds or profits go to a cause that you could sell directly or through others.

How to come up with ideas

Brainstorm and jot down initial ideas that come to mind for meeting your goal. You don't need to scope these out in any detail yet (we'll do that in the next chapter). The first stage is to just get your ideas out of your head and onto paper as a list, Post-it™ notes or mind-map.

You could also:

- Search online, e.g. on YouTube, Google and social media platforms.

- Ask your contacts, clients, followers and business partners for their ideas (this can sometimes be a really powerful way to connect and engage with your community).

- Participate in others' fundraising events.

- Copy what you see others doing well.

- Activate the right side of your brain – draw, mind-map, exercise or do another creative activity.

- Tap into universal intelligence and collective consciousness e.g. through meditation or other techniques you use for this.

- If you want to raise funds for a cause through your business, remember to check out Chapter 4, which is packed with ideas.

Your ideas shortlist

Once you've come up with some ideas, it's time to pick your favourites before scoping them out further and deciding which to go with, which we'll do in the next chapter.

Key Points

💗 If you want to meet your goals, in a way that makes best use of resources, and doesn't distract you from other business activities, it's well worth taking the time to brainstorm ideas before deciding which to implement.

💗 Remember you're looking to come up with ideas you, your business and social causes will all benefit from.

 Social Impact Actions

Jot down available resources and initial ideas in your the Give-to-Profit Practical Guide that accompanies this book. If you've not already got it, you can download it for free at www.givetoprofit.com.

Optimise Your Impact

*"What's the point in being alive if you don't try
to make things better?"*

JK ROWLING, AUTHOR

Whether or not you're consciously aware of it, you impact the lives of others with every encounter. But are you having the kind of impact you'd like?

It only takes a few strategic tweaks to turn a small idea into one that has far more impact. The purpose of this chapter is to introduce you to a simple 'Seven-Plus-Win' model you can use to leverage your resources for the greatest positive impact and return on your investment. I'm sharing this model in the context of achieving a charitable goal, but you can use this to develop and monetise other business ideas too.

A few years ago I decided to support the launch of a book written by one of my friends, David Hamilton. I'd organised lots of workshops and events for David and we could have followed the same formula as before with David doing a short talk and selling books.

But because the book accompanied the global release of a film, we felt this warranted more of a celebration.

Leverage your time and available resources for maximum impact

By applying the 'Seven-Plus-Win' model described in this chapter, a book-signing turned into a fundraising film premiere, with a red-carpet drinks reception for over 100 people. In doing so we had a fabulous evening and raised more than US$1,000 for charity. This meant we were able to sponsor a Project Ambassador in Rwanda for a year. Business-wise I raised my visibility and attracted new clients, as did David. I'll reveal more about what we did shortly.

Expand your ideas: the 'Seven-Plus-Win' model

You've probably heard of the concept of coming up with a win-win solution – one where both parties benefit. And you may also have heard of win-win-win solutions where a three parties benefit. But what if you could help more people?

That's what the 'Seven-Plus-Win' model does. It helps you consider how you can make small tweaks to your idea so it has a positive impact on at least seven groups of people. What you do is consider your idea from a number of different perspectives, as summarised in the diagram on the opposite page:

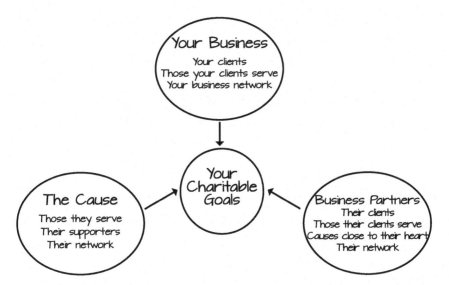

The diagram above highlights the more immediate parties who could benefit from giving through your business including:

- Your business (your vision, goals, products, services, marketing, etc.)

- Your clients

- Those your clients serve

- Your business network

- Your business partners

- Causes your business partners support

- Your business partners' clients

- Those your partners' clients serve

- Your business partners' network or community

- The charity or cause

- Those the cause serves

- Those who support the cause.

Yes OK, I realise there are more than seven perspectives in the list above but not all of these will apply to each idea. However, by considering how to touch the lives of each of these clusters, you're likely to have more impact than had you not done this. It's fairly easy to come up with seven plus groups of people benefiting from your efforts. And remember there will be a ripple effect too that means you'll impact indirectly the lives of many more people.

Wearing the hats of each of the above groups of people, ask yourself the following questions:

- How could I help or add value to XXX?

- How could I have more of a positive impact for XXX?

- How could XXX help me have greater impact?

- What would make this more appealing to XXX?

- How could I raise more funds from this idea?

- How could I be of greater service?

- How could this have an ongoing positive impact?

- What are the benefits for XXX if they participate?

- What are the implications of XXX participating?

- What would XXX really like?

By reviewing your ideas from these different perspectives, you'll come up with better thought-out solutions.

Having asked the above questions in relation to David's book launch, we made a few changes to the event:

- We decided to run a film premiere rather than a talk launching a book.

- We focused on giving attendees the special experience of attending a film premiere (with red carpet), a great night out, plus the chance to meet the author and network with each other.

- We raised funds by charging an entrance fee, selling my miracle bracelets and raffle tickets.

- We gathered support from clients and contacts in our networks who donated prizes for the raffle, and promoted the event.

One of the lovely things that happened that night was two of the attendees winning the prize the other had donated into the raffle. They subsequently met up and went on to collaborate in various ways. Like anything else in life, you just don't know what could happen when you say 'yes' to an opportunity.

We could possibly have raised a similar amount for charity by sticking to the formula of a talk and raffle but with a little bit of extra effort we made it a special night for everyone there. Because we'd expanded the vision yet wanted to keep it manageable too, we asked others to help out on the night.

I loved an 'ah-ha' moment one of my clients had during a live Give-to-Profit event, after I'd presented this model – that business partners don't have to be other businesses; charities and social causes could be great collaborative business partners too.

Monetise your ideas

Since the context of what I teach in this book is to grow your business by supporting social causes, it's important to consider also how you can monetise each of your ideas – now and in the future. This relates to maximising financial gains for your business as well as the social cause you're supporting.

Monetising your ideas for your business

Remember the example I gave about the fundraising event I ran to raise funds for a trip to Rwanda that resulted in an unexpected increase in ongoing monthly revenue?

While my primary goal was to raise funds to go to Rwanda, by clarifying my desired outcomes I chose a topic for my training that I thought lots of people would be interested in, and one I could potentially earn money from in the future. I didn't anticipate the monthly revenue from the attendees of that first group, but by being present and listening to what they said they wanted, I was able to make the most of the opportunity.

To make the most of fundraising events:

*   Deliver more than attendees expect.

*   Collect contact details for everyone who signs up and add them to an appropriate email list (obviously only where you have their permission to do so).

- Consider how to build up relationships with new contacts after the event to increase the likelihood they'll buy from you in the future.

- Consider what products or services attendees could be interested in after the event.

- Gather interest for other products and services at events, e.g. what people say during your event, in a chat thread (online events) or on their feedback forms.

  Personally, I never do a sales pitch during fundraiser events. Yes, during the course of an event I may share stories about how I've helped people or comment on products or services I offer. But these are passing comments rather than going into any detail of what I offer – unless someone asks for further details when of course I'll answer if the rest of the group is interested, or suggest we have a one-to-one conversation later.

- Follow up all sales leads, and let them know how you can help them with suitable products or services.

Monetising your ideas for social causes

There are several ways to maximise your social impact.

If your goal is to raise as much funds as possible, select highly attractive events, campaigns or products your ideal clients are most likely to sign up to, i.e. the ones with the highest likely demand. And review your ideas through the filter of the 'Seven-Plus-Win' model.

Consider whether there are other social causes which could also benefit from your event, e.g. by sourcing social suppliers, inviting social causes to participate, or having attendees vote on a cause they'd like to benefit.

Simplify your ideas

Having undertaken many charitable activities, I've found that the simplest ideas are both the easiest to implement, and often generate the best returns of investment for all concerned. Especially when these ideas give you the opportunity to engage with others, and can easily be integrated into existing business activities.

It can be tempting to spend lots of time on charitable activities but if you need to earn money from your business, it's important to keep your ideas simple so you can continue to focus on income-generating activities too. The simpler your ideas, the less likely your business will suffer.

Before I added this reality check to my ideas, I did fine most of the time; however, I also made a couple of decisions that cost me financially, had a negative impact on my business, and caused my health to suffer. I'm not someone who harbours regrets; but with hindsight, I know that if I'd done what I suggest in this chapter, I would not have run my Give-to-Profit Fundraising Tele-Summit a few years ago. Organising a tele-summit works for some people, though at that stage of my business, I didn't have the skills, time and technology to do this well, without my health and bank balance suffering. Yes, there were many benefits that came from the summit – it helped me clarify my message, build relationships with many wonderful new clients and partners who resonated with my vision, and it raised my visibility. But it was also a huge distraction from my business that ultimately cost me money.

There were other ways I could have raised more funds with far less effort and stress. That said, my experience shaped what I share in this book so that you avoid making the same mistakes I've

The return on your charitable giving activities is important

made! That's why I urge you to consider available resources, review all your ideas through the different perspectives and to simplify them as much as possible.

At the heart of keeping things simple is remembering to be compassionate to yourself not just others. Lots of people who support social causes find it easy to be loving, kind and compassionate towards others but are not always good about adopting this approach towards themselves. For instance they may help others at a cost to themselves; work excessively long hours; give their inner critic a voice; not look after themselves physically, spiritually or emotionally; spend too much time doing activities they don't like, or being around toxic people.

I used to live that way a lot but now practice simplicity and self-compassion at every opportunity, including when making business decisions. This involves asking for help, saying no, practicing self-care and investing in support and software to make things easier. When you look after yourself properly you can be a better support to others.

I've found the best time to do a Simplicity Health Check is after an idea has been fully scoped out. I liken this to the safety checks pilots carry out just before the start of a flight. Since putting this extra check in place, I now make smarter choices. Ask yourself:

- How could I simplify this idea?

- How could I streamline or automate processes for this idea?

- How could others help with implementing this?

- How could I be more compassionate towards myself?

- What negative impact could this idea have on my life or business?

- How could I prevent this having a negative impact on my life or business?

- Is there a better idea that could deliver at least the same outcomes for less effort (or cost)?

The last question acts as a final check if you have one idea to implement or helps you compare different ideas for achieving your charitable goal.

Decide which idea to implement

Once you've expanded, monetised and simplified each potential idea, it's time to decide which one to go with. To do this, consider each idea through the filters of the critical success factors you defined for your charitable goal (in Chapter 8). These will help you decide which of your ideas is the best fit for achieving your charitable goal.

Plan to succeed

Obviously once you've decided which idea to implement the next step is to pull together a plan to make this happen. One that lists and prioritises required actions, allocates resources and integrates your charitable activities into other business processes (where relevant).

Key Points

- With only a few small tweaks you could turn a good idea into a great one and in doing so have more social impact.

- Applying the 'Seven-Plus-Win' model will help expand the scope of ideas for greater impact, and tap into the resources of others who can help.

- Considering how to monetise your ideas for your business and social cause, is an important aspect of setting any fundraising goals.

- If you want to do this with minimal disruption to your personal life and business, also consider how you can simplify your ideas.

- To increase your likelihood of success, have a plan and integrate this into your usual business activities.

Resources

You'll find templates to help you scope out your idea and select the best way forward in The Give-to-Profit Practical Guide that accompanies this book. You can download this guide for free at www.givetoprofit.com.

12

Measure Your Impact

"Impact is the measureable difference you create in people's lives."
WENDY LIPTON-DIBNER, CHANGE-MAKER and AUTHOR

I love the quote above and particularly one important word when it comes to business success and charitable giving: *measurable.*

How do you know the difference you're making if you don't *measure* the *impact* of your activities?

I don't mean simply keeping records of what you're doing but rather measuring the benefits of your work: how your charitable activities are changing lives, or the planet.

Is it possible to know the real impact you're having? Quite simply – no, you'll never know the full extent of your impact, as relatively few people come back and tell you. And there's always a ripple effect to your actions. However, there are some things you can do to evaluate your social impact.

> *The value of your giving is only as good as the impact you have.*

The value of your giving is only as good as the impact you have. In the same way charities and social causes are either effective (or not) at utilising resources, so are businesses. This includes when they implement giving strategies.

The value of your giving

Recently I heard about a charity ball a business organised. While it was lovely that they committed to raise funds for their charity of the year, the event took months to plan and cost the same financially to host as it generated from ticket sales. They did raise funds with a raffle but there didn't seem to be any other business benefit, and they may have been better making a financial donation, or just running a raffle without the ball, and saved themselves a lot of effort.

I don't share this to put you off organising fundraising balls but rather to highlight that there's more to making a difference than good intentions. It's also important to make smart choices about how you support social causes, and to measure your impact after each charitable activity. Doing this enables you to evaluate the extent to which your efforts have been worthwhile and to determine which are the activities that generate the best social return on your investment: for you, your business and social cause. Measuring your impact will also give you meaningful data to take into account to enable you to make informed decisions in the future about which activities to continue, refine, repeat or stop doing.

Measuring your impact or *return on social investment* also gives you valuable information you can share with third parties – your clients, contacts, leads, partners and others interested in your social impact practices. This is known as impact reporting: communicating the difference you are making to those you have pledged to help or a situation you are working towards improving.

As I've mentioned previously, we're living in a time when consumers are putting pressure on businesses to 'do the right thing' and consider the social impact of their actions. Many consumers prefer to buy from companies who value (and can demonstrate) their social impact. In the last month alone I've heard of two mobile apps being developed that track individuals' social impact.

Likewise, some organisations prefer to buy from, or partner with, other businesses who can demonstrate the difference they are making. For example, in the UK it's common practice for businesses bidding for public-sector contracts to be asked to share their social impact policies (and how they evidence this) as part of their tender.

Proactively sharing your social impact demonstrates your level of commitment to make a difference and be transparent. When done well, this can help influence your brand and 'story' and the business you attract.

What to measure

The variables to define and measure are those that demonstrate the benefits of your charitable activities – for you personally, your business and charitable causes.

Measuring personal benefits is obviously a subjective exercise and involves taking the time to reflect on this. By contrast, measuring the impact for your business and cause is more objective and can be done by defining key performance indicators (KPIs) to measure regularly.

In Chapter 8 I suggested identifying critical success factors when defining your charitable goal, to use to help you select the best charitable activities to pursue. Now you can review these and decide which would be most valuable in measuring your impact. In other words you can convert some of these factors into KPIs against which you can measure the social impact of your charitable giving.

Business impact

It's prudent to measure key KPIs for your business irrespective of any charitable giving. Here, all we're doing is also extracting results relating specifically to your charitable activities. These could include:

- Value of sales and profit

- Number of referrals

- Leads and clients – number and value

- Visibility, e.g. social media followers

- Engagement with your audience, clients and business network

- New opportunities to share your story (e.g. through interviews or speaking engagements).

If you have been fundraising through your business, make sure you monitor and report all relevant information for any 'cause marketing' legislation that applies to you (see Chapter 5).

Charitable impact

Examples of KPIs you could use to measure how your activities have benefited your cause of choice include:

- Value of funds donated or raised

- How specifically the lives of those you intend to help have been changed

- Life-stories from beneficiaries that provide evidence of the impact of your charitable activities

- Impact statistics, e.g. number of lives saved, people rescued, cured or employed

- Quotes, testimonials and feedback from volunteers and beneficiaries, on the difference your support has made

- Messages of thanks – from beneficiaries and volunteers

- Results of surveys – you do with those you're aiming to help

- Number of days you've volunteered or donated your time

- Increased visibility (e.g. more media coverage or a greater presence on social media platforms)

- New funding opportunities or grants

- New supporters who pledge regular donations

- New supporters on their database

- Resources the cause could use to generate future income

- New volunteers, board members, ambassadors or strategic partners.

Be mindful that recording what you're doing, for example how much you raise or donate, is useful data but may be more a measure of your contribution and results, rather than the *actual impact* you have had.

Focus on impact

There is a difference between your contribution and your social impact. Raising funds, donating money and supporting a cause is only part of the story: how these resources are put to use also matters. In other words, being able to determine how your efforts have actually changed lives, saved lives, helped people increase their income, get jobs, etc.

There is a difference between your contribution and your social impact.

If you're supporting a cause that can tell you, for example, how many meals, school uniforms, mosquito nets or trees every few pounds or dollars buys, it's easy to gather, record and share this information. The causes may also have further information on the ripple effects of how these resources have changed lives or improved the planet.

When deciding what to measure, it may also be worth considering what your audience want to know, and making sure you collate robust information that demonstrates this.

How to measure your impact

Once you've identified the key factors to measure it's a case of integrating these into any business reporting processes you already have and allocating resources to do this effectively. The easiest way is to set up a spreadsheet to record targets, activities and results for any relevant period – unless you've got a good software solution for doing this.

With advances in technology we're starting to see software that enables consumers and those supporting causes to track their impact using software and apps. For example the social enterprise *From Me to We* enables their customers to track their impact through their website.

If you're already regularly measuring and reviewing the performance of your business, e.g. reviewing key performance indicators monthly, quarterly or annually, simply update these to reflect your charitable activities.

The extent to which you need to monitor, evaluate and evidence your social impact depends on your business, the contracts you have, and any relevant legislation. That said, it's good business practice to do this whether or not you are required to do so.

Impact reporting

Whether you're obliged to share your results and impact with others, or you choose to do this voluntarily, the next stage is to decide how to do this – both with those who work in your business and externally.

You can collate and present this information in a number of different formats:

- Written reports – including key data, trends, images, interviews and written commentary.

- Info-graphics

- Images

- Videos.

You will find more about how to communicate to others and weave your impact into your story in the next chapter.

There are many large charities and social causes that do this really well, so if you want to see examples of what you could do, it's worth checking out a few of your favourite causes to see what they do – on their websites and social media platforms. You can often also download copies of reports from them too.

In the same way, I suggest integrating the gathering of key data into your internal performance management processes; consider how you can also feed your charitable impact results into your communication and marketing strategies.

Transparency

It's also worth considering how you can be open with the causes you support, your customers, partners and followers.

Sharing results and information with them goes part of the way but the scope of being transparent is broader than sharing information. It also involves the full disclosure of things like your business ethics and values, how robust your systems and processes are, disclosure of any 'material' facts or potential conflicts of interest, and how proactive you are in sharing all this information.

One of the ways I've aimed to be transparent with my fundraising was to set up a fundraising page with a fundraising portal so people could see me processing donations and the main charity I was supporting also knew what I had raised. If you want to do this, just do an Internet search for 'giving portal' and you'll find plenty to choose from.

Key Points

- The value of your giving is only as good as the impact you have – raising funds, donating money and supporting a cause is only part of the story: how these resources are put to use also matters.

Increasingly, potential customers and business partners choose to do business with those who can demonstrate they are doing good in the world. So make sure you have robust and meaningful information you can share with them.

Get creative with ways of demonstrating your impact and create content in a range of different formats.

Integrate how you measure your charitable activities into your business management reporting, communication and marketing strategies.

If you're fundraising through your business, remember to check out any 'cause marketing' reporting and transparency requirements that apply to you (see chapter 5).

 Social Impact Actions

- Decide how you're going to evaluate the results of your charitable activities and what you'd like to share with your clients or followers.

- Check out how charities and social causes you like are providing evidence of their impact, for inspiration.

- Note your ideas in the Give-to-Profit Practical Guide that accompanies this book, downloadable free at www.givetoprofit.com.

13

Share Your Story

"After nourishment, shelter and companionship, stories are the thing we need most in the world."

PHILIP PULLMAN, AUTHOR

I was saddened to hear about the death of the pop star Prince but also pleasantly surprised to hear about all social projects he was involved in. Activities he proactively kept quiet while he was alive.

Opinions are divided on whether to tell others about any charitable work you do.

I, like many others, feel really inspired and uplifted when I hear about people who help others in need or take action to protect parts of the planet, cultures or traditions I've not thought about before. Why? Because I'm interested in people and all that lives on this planet; it's good to be reminded that most people are kind at heart and that we are human beings living on a constantly evolving planet with many different forms of life.

I love hearing about the scope of work being done by amazing people and causes. Their work and stories often stimulate ideas in my mind and inspire me into action. Hearing others' stories helps me maintain a better and more balanced view of world affairs – that despite the plethora of bad news stories in the media, there's a lot of love and good happening too.

But I also hear some people saying they admire people more for keeping charitable giving quiet – as though it's better not to tell anyone.

Sharing your story helps you attract the right clients, staff and business opportunities

How much you share with others is personal and needs to be aligned to what feels right to you. However, if you decide to keep quiet about your charitable giving, do so in the knowledge that you're not helping your chosen social cause as much as you could. And doing so might also hinder your ability to grow business by supporting social causes. It could even send potential customers to your competition – customers who deliberately buy from companies and brands that are public about their charitable giving.

Remember charities and social causes need your support. They need people like you to be out spreading the word about their good work in a competitive world. They may not be in 'business' but they are competing for support. One of the reasons charities appoint celebrity ambassadors is that this type of endorsement gives them more visibility, which they hope will attract more supporters and funders.

To help guide you, on what is right for you ask yourself the following questions:

* How could my cause benefit from me telling others about my support?

- In what way is it in the cause's best interest for me to keep quiet about what I'm doing?

Sharing your story raises the profile of the causes you support

- What part is my ego playing in influencing what I'm doing (including worrying about what others think)?

What is your story?

Over time, each individual charitable action and outcome becomes part of your story and influences what you're known for (your brand).

- Why is supporting social causes important to you?

- How have you supported social causes to date?

- What plans do you have for the future?

- What results and outcomes have you experienced?

- What community, following or movement are you building in relation to this?

- How has supporting charitable causes changed you or shaped your business?

- What key insights or messages could inspire others?

When you get involved in charitable activities at a practical level such as volunteering your time, or talking about your experiences, you'll bring the story alive more quickly.

What to share

This depends on the particular activities you choose to do, the extent to which you integrate these into your business, the brand you want to build, and any regulatory requirements, particularly if you are fundraising (see Chapter 5). You could share:

- Details of your events or campaigns, e.g. dates, targets, progress updates, amount raised, etc.

- Reasons why you are doing this

- Images

- Results, outcomes and success stories (as they happen or as part of a regular impact report)

- Videos of people who have benefited from your support

- Case studies of those who have benefited from your work (where you have permission to share these)

- Quotes or testimonials from those you've helped

- Comments or testimonials from those you've collaborated with

- Comments or words of thanks from the social causes

- Your own thoughts, reflections or experiences

- Information about the social causes you are supporting

- The Give-to-Profit Pledge – see below.

Obviously if you're sharing any personal stories, details, or photos of others make sure you get written permission from them beforehand and that you comply with relevant data-protection legislation. Likewise, it would be wise to check with any relevant cause in advance that they are happy for you to publically mention what you're doing.

Ways to share your story

This relates to how you share your story with others – both internally with your team or colleagues, causes you support and externally with others.

A good place to start is to reflect your charitable giving, story and impact in what you're already doing for your business. This could include:

- In your marketing material or promotional literature

- A giving or social impact page on your website

- In blogs or vlogs (video blogs)

- Across social media platforms

- When networking

- In your books

- In staff policies (if you have them)

- In your places of work or team meetings.

Once you've updated existing business practices, consider how you could share your story more widely:

- In press releases

- Give talks or presentations

- Through partners, e.g. in interviews, special appearances or guest blogging.

Build a community or movement

Ideas and visions that capture the hearts and minds of others have the potential to become a movement: a community of people with similar thoughts or values who come together to collectively influence change.

In recent years around the world we've experienced movements of different guises all challenging the 'establishment', distribution of wealth and globalisation: in the Middle East these movements have taken the form of uprisings and civil wars while in the West we've had the Brexit vote in the UK, and Donald Trump becoming the US president. What started as people sharing the same views coming together became a swell that rocked the boat – for good or bad.

Your story becomes part of what you're known for: your personal and business brand. This in turn attracts new followers, staff, clients or partners who resonate with your message and the social impact you're having through your business.

You don't have to lead a movement – you may prefer to be part of others' movements for example the Give-to-Profit movement or to grow your own community and see how others respond to your ideas.

However, if you have a vision to build a movement, be mindful of this from the outset, when crafting your story and which strategies you use to do this.

- What do you want to be known for?

- What do you want your business to stand for?

- Does your charitable giving form part of this?

- Would you like to lead a movement for positive change?

- Or would you prefer be part of another movement?

The Give-to-Profit Pledge

These are basic guiding principles I put at the heart of my business and communicate to others through my marketing. The principles I commit to through this pledge include:

- I always aim to interact with people and the planet from a place of love, kindness and compassion in my heart, as I write about in my book *Heartatude: The 9 Principles of Heart-Centered Success.*

- To me there's more to business than simply making money – I also aim to make the world a better place through my business.

- I support social causes through my business and apply best practices when doing so.

What would you like to publically pledge to the world?

If the above statements strike a chord with you, once you've finished reading this book I invite you to join the growing movement of people who are committing to support social causes through their business. You can find out more about the Give-to-Profit Pledge on my website www.givetoprofit.com.

Key Points

As a small business owner, when you share the social impact you're having through your business, this becomes part of your brand and helps you stand out from the crowd.

❤ Stories sell, and so does demonstrating you care.

❤ Social causes need people like you to tell others how you're supporting them. Keeping your business charitable giving quiet isn't helping social causes (and those they serve) as much as you could.

❤ Share the social impact you are having as you go along both internally with your staff or team, causes you support and externally through your communication and marketing strategies.

 Social Impact Actions

- Note ideas for how you could document and share your story in your Give-to-Profit Guide.

- Ask social causes you support how they'd like you to become an ambassador for them, so more people know about their work.

- Regularly review and update your story.

- Decide which movements you'd like to lead or participate in. If you'd like to become part of the Give-to-Profit movement sign up to the Give-to-Profit Pledge at www.givetoprofit.com.

What You Do Next Matters!

"An Ordinary Person Can Create Extraordinary Change."

ADAM BRAUN, FOUNDER of PENCILS of PROMISE

Imagine your business having the impact you'd like it to have. How this would change or add meaning your life?

One of the most memorable and life changing moments I've experienced in Rwanda was when we told one of the genocide survivors we'd been helping, that a high profile American philanthropist had offered to give us money to buy her a house.

Thanks to the generosity of many people around the world, this has been just one of the miracles experienced by those who benefit from our work. What made this one so memorable was the sequence of events and little actions that had resulted in this happening.

Chantal was the first young person in Rwanda I sponsored. As a young girl of eight at the time of the genocide she'd witnessed her family being murdered in front of her, then left for dead in a mass grave. Fortunately she was able to climb out and hide before being rescued a few days later. Like many other orphaned children she'd learnt to fend for herself over the years but was still highly traumatised and living in squalid conditions in a Kigali slum.

When Chantal joined our Project Light Program (trauma healing, heart-centered leadership and entrepreneurial training) she was a keen yet quiet participator still trapped in the horrors of her memories. However, it didn't take long for her to release the trauma associated with her memories and to believe in the possibility she could enjoy a very different life – depending on what action she took next. Chantal decided to open a shop – or rather to start selling critical goods from the steps of her one-roomed home. Soon she had made enough money to buy a mattress, a chair and other comforts most of us take for granted, yet many people around the world don't have. She was also making smart business decisions like moving to a larger home where one of the rooms could be a shop, then buying a TV and chairs so people would come to her shop to watch it, and buy from her at the same time. This was followed by a fridge/freezer she used to chill drinks and keep medicines cool, which again attracted more customers. Fairly quickly it was evident that Chantal is a natural entrepreneur and it was lovely to see her becoming a respected leader in her community.

However, some didn't like her success: namely her landlords who upon seeing her success wanted a piece of it for themselves. Three times she was evicted and had to start again – in a new home and area. This was why I decided to run my Give-to-Profit summit in 2014 – I'd hoped to raise the US$25,000 we needed to buy her a house, so she could enjoy more stability in her life. She still experiences awful headaches from the attacks endured during the genocide and I wanted her to have a comfortable home she could feel safe and secure in, and from which she could make a living. However, as I shared in earlier chapters, this was my one attempt at fundraising that didn't work.

Fast forward a few months and I'm back in Rwanda having a discussion with another two team members, Lori and Rosemary. We decided that together we would raise the money to build Chantal a house. Rather than focussing on how we'd do this, we meditated on this happening easily and effortlessly. I'm sure you can imagine our stunned excitement when we received a phone message the very next morning that a philanthropist had heard about our quest to build Chantal a house, and he wanted to give us the money.

> *Your future and that of your business depends on what you do next.*

Obviously there were far more people involved in that happening, it was the culmination of many single actions and tiny steps we'd taken over the years. And that's the point – you can create whatever type of business and social impact you'd like in the world when you consistently take action aligned to your goals and dreams.

You don't need to choose between financial success and what's important to you – you can have a commercial business that is aligned to your values. Nor do you need to set up a charity, foundation or social enterprise to have social impact through your business: the Give-to-Profit model enables you to combine charitable giving and a commercial business. Even if you're new in business there are plenty ways to grow your business by supporting social causes. You don't need to wait until your business is successful.

Your future and that of your business depends on what you do next. You could keep all your ideas from reading this book in your head but that wouldn't help anyone. Or you could take inspired action to bring them to life and make a difference in the world – in whatever way works for you. Remember there is a huge difference between having good intentions and having a positive impact.

In the case of Chantal, many of us had been doing all sorts of things over the years to raise visibility of our work in Rwanda, and as a consequence we have quite a few high profile supporters. We kept the dream of what could happen alive and invited others to participate in turning these possibilities into reality, while also letting go of how this would happen. On Chantal's part, she had never heard of the person who made the donation but consistently took action towards her dream, overcoming many hurdles and not giving up. She also had the opportunity and courage to share her dream of owning her own home with us. None of us knew how exactly we'd raise the cash, but we didn't need to. It's often easier to achieve goals when you get clarity on what they are, and simply start by taking steps aligned to these, while at the same time let go of the need to know how they will manifest.

Whatever you decide to do, I invite you to:

- Keep your ideas simple – start with the easiest ideas that will make the biggest difference to you, your business and cause. You can always change, refine or expand upon your charitable giving later.

- Plan to succeed – set yourself a charitable goal and allocate time, money or resources to this. The free Give-to-Profit Practical Guide that accompanies this book is designed to help you consolidate and implement your ideas. You can download this guide for free and find out other useful resources, including the Give-to-Profit community, at www. givetoprofit.com.

- Take action – commit to taking your first step today whether to put a date in your diary for a fundraiser event, to develop a plan, to speak to a cause you'd like to support or to join our community.

Remember, charities and social causes need your support; consumers prefer to buy from businesses that care about their social impact; and charitable giving can help you grow your business. You're also likely to feel a deeper sense of meaning and fulfilment in your work when you incorporate charitable giving into your business.

What are you going to do next to make a difference in the world?

12G2P2017

An Invitation to Connect

"Feeling good about your life but not expressing a heartfelt thank you
is like wrapping a gift for someone and
never giving it to them."

CHIP CONLEY, ENTREPRENEUR

Thanks for taking the time to read this book. I hope it's inspired you to turn your business into a force for good in whatever way lights up your heart.

None of us in isolation can save the world but through every decision you make, you can help make it a better place. You're already making a difference just by being here today and can have even more impact when you implement ideas you've had while reading this book.

I invite you to join the growing community of compassionate business owners and entrepreneurs around the world who are embracing social giving as part of their business – together we are co-creating a powerful ripple of change.

I'd love to hear what you think about this book and what you're doing to have greater social impact – so please do get in touch and let me know.

It would be great if you could also take a moment to review this book on Amazon, and to tell others about it so we can touch the lives of more people. Thank you!

With love and light,

Alisoun x

I'd love to hear your thoughts, questions and success stories. Check out www.alisoun.com for details of how to connect with me, get support or have me speak at one of your events.

And remember to check out all the free resources that accompany this book at www.givetoprofit.com.

Dedication

This book is dedicated to my husband Paul Winkle who has lovingly supported my desire to do humanitarian work, helped me think bigger and so much more. Thank you!

Gratitude

There are so many people who have been part of my business and humanitarian journey over the last few years to whom I'm eternally grateful. You know who you are and I'm sending a huge hug of thanks your way now!

I'd especially like to thank all those who have supported my fundraising efforts, embraced Give-to-Profit for themselves and in particular the following people who have been a huge influence on the content of this book – my mum for editing it (you've been an amazing editor); Jennifer Main who suggested the scope of Give-to-Profit was bigger than I'd thought (you were right); my dearest friend Lori Leyden for continually inspiring me through the work we do in Rwanda; Kim and Sinclair Macleod of Indie Authors World for bringing Give-to-Profit to life (in their own business as well as publishing this book); the speakers on my Give-to-Profit summit who helped stimulate ideas for what this could become; and to all those who've helped me refine the content.

With lots of love

Alisoun x

About Alisoun Mackenzie

The Compassionate Business Mentor

"Business is a great opportunity to be kind"

Alisoun Mackenzie

Often described as one of the most authentic and inspiring souls you can meet, Alisoun is on a mission to guide heart-centered business owners and entrepreneurs to turn their passions into profits and make a difference in the world.

Her entrepreneurial spark was lit when she launched a travel club in 1991, and became a new way of life in 2003 when she left the investment industry to start her own business.

Since then Alisoun's keynote presentations, training events, mentoring and her best-selling book, *Heartatude, The 9 Principles of Heart-Centered Success*, have favorably changed the good fortune of thousands of people worldwide.

Alisoun's regular humanitarian trips to Rwanda, helping young genocide survivors, have profoundly changed her life, and influenced the way she puts social impact at the core of her business.

She is full of gratitude everyday for the joyful and meaningful life she leads – living near a beach just outside Edinburgh, Scotland.

Alisoun's first best-selling book:

Heartatude, The 9 Principles of Heart-Centered Success

"Be ready to enjoy a journey that will touch your heart and open your mind to new possibilities."

Dr David Hamilton, Scientist, Author And Speaker

Is there anything in your life you'd love to change?
Do you have a goal or dream you'd love to achieve?
Would you like to cope better with life's challenges?

This best-selling book will show you how to make this happen.

You are living in one of the most exciting times of human history – with a wealth of wisdom, resources, and opportunities available to help you create a happy, successful, and meaningful life

Heartatude, offers an authentic, compassionate, and holistic approach for putting yourself in the best place to do this, and make a difference to others. Packed with ancient wisdom, science, transformational tools, practical tips, and inspirational stories, The 9 Principles of Heart-Centered Success are the key for attracting more happiness and success – in all areas of life.

Read Heartatude and discover what miracles await you...

It's Possible! You Can Do It! You Deserve It!

Invite Alisoun to speak at one of your events!

Alisoun is an inspiring and engaging Keynote Speaker and welcomes invitations to speak at conferences and events around the world. Her Keynote Talks include:

- Give-to-Profit: How to Grow Your Business by Supporting Charities and Social Causes

- How to Turn Your Events into Fun Fundraisers

- From Stockbroker to Humanitarian: Adventures in Authentic Living

- The Compassionate Sales Formula

- Embrace Possibility and Success

> *"Alisoun's talks are engaging, relevant and interesting, and always straight from the heart. Highly recommended!"*
>
> Mel Sherwood, Pitch & Presentation Specialist,
> President The Professional Speakers Association, Scotland 2016-17

To find out more contact Alisoun via www.alisoun.com

Work with Alisoun

Business Mentoring and Executive Coaching

Alisoun helps heart-centered business owners, entrepreneurs and visionary leaders to turn their passions into profits and make a difference in the world.

Give-to-Profit Talks

As an inspiring and engaging Keynote Speaker, Alisoun welcomes invitations to speak at conferences and client events around the world.

Training Consultancy and Courses

Alisoun offers training solutions to universities, business networks and service providers who value social impact and want to include Give-to-Profit in their courses and training programs. She also runs a training academy for business owners and entrepreneurs.

Give-to-Profit Consultancy Services

Alisoun works with clients on a consultancy basis to help them implement their charitable giving ideas into their business strategy and to incorporate fundraising elements into their conferences and events.

Partner with Alisoun

Alisoun loves to collaborate with other business leaders and social entrepreneurs.

To find out more contact Alisoun via www.alisoun.com

The Compassionate Sales Formula

Do you hate or avoid selling, yet want more clients?

If yes that's likely to be because you're got negative thoughts and feelings about selling, or you don't know how to sign up clients in a way that's aligned to your values.

I used to feel that way too until I realised selling is an opportunity to be kind – especially when you align your marketing and selling to what's important to you.

The Compassionate Sales Formula gives you the confidence to SIGN UP more CLIENTS in a way that's KIND, AUTHENTIC and FEELS GOOD!

By completing this course you will learn how to:

- Adopt a positive mindset to selling, money and success

- Promote yourself authentically and generate plenty leads

- Put compassionate sales funnels in place that generate plenty clients

- Follow up the leads and build great relationships

- Structure client conversations in a way that feels good and has people saying 'yes' to you more often

- Create a robust sales action plan to follow.

Are you ready to turn your dreams into reality?

To find out more about this and other training courses offered by Alisoun, go to www.alisoun.com

Lightning Source UK Ltd.
Milton Keynes UK
UKOW05f0614290317
297789UK00017B/353/P